Stadium Stories:
New York Giants

Stadium Stories™ Series

Stadium Stories:
New York Giants

Michael Eisen

INSIDERS' GUIDE®

GUILFORD, CONNECTICUT
AN IMPRINT OF THE GLOBE PEQUOT PRESS

INSIDERS' GUIDE®

Text design: Casey Shain
All photos courtesy of Jerry Pinkus, unless otherwise noted.
Cover photos: *front cover:* Phil Simms; *back cover:* top, Lawrence Taylor; bottom, Giants Stadium (New York Giants).

Library of Congress Cataloging-in-Publication Data is available.

ISBN 0-7627-3778-6

Manufactured in the United States of America
First Edition/Third Printing

I would like to dedicate this book to my family: my wife, Karen, who is a great friend, loyal supporter, good-natured critic, and loving partner; Molly, a beautiful and bright young woman; Harrison, who loves all sports and especially the Giants; and Isabel, the cutest and chattiest little girl in the world.

Contents

Acknowledgments

This book would not have come to life without the assistance and support of many people, and I would like to thank them.

Jim Buckley and Jim Gigliotti approached me about writing the book and then convinced me to do it. Mary Norris and Mike Urban of The Globe Pequot Press were extremely helpful. I particularly appreciate everyone's flexibility and understanding regarding deadlines.

Many members of the Giants organization were helpful and supportive, including John Mara, Rusty Hawley, and Pat Hanlon. Doug Murphy and Jerry Pinkus provided invaluable assistance in finding and transmitting the photographs. Phyllis Hayes and Karen Eisen provided enormous assistance by transcribing taped interviews. Steve Venditti generously made his office available so I could view videotapes.

I would also like to thank everyone who was generous enough to talk to me and provided so many great stories for this book, including Wellington Mara, Frank Gifford, Sam Huff, Pat Summerall, Ed Croke, Dick Nolan, Allie Sherman, Phil Simms, George Martin, Harry Carson, Brian Kelley, Brad Van Pelt, Lawrence Taylor, Carl Banks, Brad Benson, Bill Ard, Jim Fassel, Michael Strahan, Tiki Barber, and Jason Sehorn.

Introduction

The 2005 season will be my twentieth being close to the Giants, either as a reporter covering the team or as a member of the organization. But my connection to the team goes back much further than that.

I have been following the team for as long as I can remember. In 1968, when I was twelve years old, I attended a Giants game in Yankee Stadium for the first time. I was fortunate to attend many more games, and when I moved away from the metropolitan area for several years, I caught up with the Giants whenever possible in different cities.

In 1986 I was hired by the *Daily Record* in Morristown, New Jersey, to cover the Giants. My first season, the Giants won the Super Bowl. Two years later I joined the *Star-Ledger* of Newark. In 1990 I saw the Giants win another Super Bowl.

Just prior to the beginning of the 2000 season, I crossed the line and joined the Giants organization. In my initial season with the club, the Giants played in Super Bowl XXXV.

In the last two decades, I have had the privilege of witnessing unforgettable performances by great players like Lawrence Taylor, Phil Simms, Harry Carson, Joe Morris, Tiki Barber, and Michael Strahan and of seeing some of the most memorable games in Giants history, including victories in two Super Bowls and three NFC Championship Games. I've had the privilege of getting to know and becoming friends with many of the players and coaches who have come through Giants Stadium. And I have had the tremendous pleasure to work for the Mara and Tisch families, the best owners in sports.

I'm sure the next twenty years will be even better.

Wellington Mara

Let's say this right at the top: No one in the history of American sports has had a career quite like Wellington T. Mara. Quite possibly, no one in any endeavor has been as closely associated with a famed entity as long as Mara has with the New York Giants.

The 2005 season will be the Giants eighty-first in the National Football League. It will also be Mara's eighty-first with the team. Think about that—eighty-one years in the same job. Actually, Mara has had many jobs as the most important and influential figure in franchise history, as well as one of the most respected and prominent men in the history of the NFL. In 1997 Mara was elected to the Pro Football Hall of Fame, joining his father, Tim Mara, who was a charter member of the Hall. Wellington Mara attended the induction ceremony and then, as was typical of him, was back at work the next day.

That's pretty much the way it's been since 1925, when Tim Mara, a legal bookmaker and successful businessman and promoter, paid $500 to bring an NFL franchise to New York. Wellington was nine, and he soon had his first job, as a ball boy for the team. "I always enjoyed as a very young kid going to practice and being up close to the players in the locker room," Mara said. "It was a big, big thing."

It didn't take long for young Wellington to exert his influence on the franchise. The Giants lost their first two games on the road before making their home debut in the Polo Grounds on October 18, 1925. Wellington started the game in the stands with his mother, but eventually he worked his way down to the Giants' bench, where he sat with his father. His older brother Jack worked the first-down chains. "I remember hearing the coach, Bob Folwell, sending a player, Paul Jappe, into the game saying, 'Go and give them hell,'" Mara said. "And I remember thinking to myself what a rough game this must be."

Especially for a young boy who frequently suffered from colds. Then, as now, most home team benches were on the press box side of the field. Early in the game, the Giants' bench was covered in shadows, which exacerbated the cold Wellington had that day. When she saw her son sniffling at home following the Giants' 14–0 loss to the Frankford Yellow Jackets, Mrs. Mara ordered Mr. Mara to move the team's bench to the sunny side of the field. Today, eight decades later, it remains there, across the field from the press box. In the mid-1970s, coach Bill Arnsparger asked Wellington to move the bench below the press box. "The visiting team's coaches can see our sideline signals from their seats in the press box," Arnsparger said.

"Get better signals," Mara said. The Giants stayed in the sun.

Mara's influence in the organization has never wavered. In 1930 Tim turned over the ownership to his two sons, Jack, who was then twenty-two, and Wellington, who was all of fourteen. As Wellington grew, he graduated to the on-the-field operations, then to scouting and general organization, and eventually to front-office executive capacity, where he now serves as president and co-chief executive officer. The only interruption in Mara's Giants career was during World War II, when he served with distinction for more than three years in the Navy, seeing action in both the Atlantic and Pacific theaters aboard aircraft carriers and emerging as a lieutenant commander.

In addition to serving the Giants admirably for so many years, Mara has also been an invaluable contributor to the NFL as a member of many ownership committees. Indeed, he has always put the league's interests ahead of what was best for the Giants. As the NFL's flagship franchise in the nation's largest media market, the Giants could have become the league's version of the New York Yankees, rich enough to hoard the best players, while teams in smaller markets were forced to pick at the leftovers. But Mara insisted that all NFL teams equally share national television revenue, arguably the most important decision in maintaining competitive balance in the NFL.

Wellington Mara celebrates at the awards ceremony following the Giants' victory in the 2000 NFC Championship Game.

Mara is the president of the National Football Conference, and he has served on many of the NFL's influential committees. He has also been involved in every aspect of operating the Giants in their eighty-one-year existence and has been instrumental in the franchise's long list of accomplishments: twenty-six postseason appearances (the second-highest total in league history), including eighteen NFL divisional championships and six NFL championships, among them the Super Bowl XXI and Super Bowl XXV titles.

Until 1965 Wellington was responsible for the franchise's football decisions, while Jack Mara handled the business operations of the team. The Giants played in five NFL Championship Games in six seasons from 1958 to 1963, and keys to that success included trades engineered by Mara that brought Y. A. Tittle, Andy Robustelli, Del Shofner, Dick Modzelewski, Pat Summerall, Joe Walton, Dick Lynch, Erich Barnes, Bill Svoboda, Harland Svare, Bob Schnelker, Herb Rich, Ed Hughes, and Walt Yowarsky, among others, to the club. Draft choices Frank Gifford and Rosie Brown went on to become members of the Pro Football Hall of Fame (as did Tuffy Leemans, whom Wellington had recommended in 1936).

Mara has long since ceded the day-to-day running of the Giants to others, but he remains a vital and powerful presence in the franchise, and no important decision is made without his input. Through it all he has remained an extraordinarily modest and caring man who has helped many Giants during and after their playing days.

"Working for Wellington Mara is one of the treasured moments of a thirty-four-year NFL career," general manager

Ernie Accorsi said. "What a joy and a privilege. To be able to be around a virtual professional football library, a living history from the league's inception, is something I'm grateful for every day. And more important than all of that, each moment you're around Wellington Mara, you have a beacon of morality and integrity as someone to try to model yourself after."

"You see a common thread in his devotion to family and to team and to league," NFL Commissioner Paul Tagliabue said. "He has always been someone who can make everyone else better and can work with everybody. From a league perspective it's hard to imagine anyone who can be more competitive at the team level, but yet be as much as a partner—a loyal and constructive partner—at the league level. I think that's an extraordinary mark."

Wellington T. Mara was born in New York City on August 14, 1916. Although sports weren't as pervasive in society then as they are today, many of Mara's childhood memories revolved around football—and baseball. Like many New York youngsters, he was a Yankees fan.

"I remember as a kid I was taken down to the Yankees dugout and introduced to Babe Ruth and Lou Gehrig, which was a big thrill, of course," Mara said. "It was in Yankee Stadium, so I know it was after 1923. I remember one day my mother and father took me for a drive. It was a Sunday. And we went to see Yankee Stadium being completed. Then we went up to see my father's new golf club, which was Winged Foot. Both opened in 1923. I would say it was 1924 or 1925 that I got to meet Ruth and Gehrig.

"This was before you had a public-address system. The public-address system consisted of one or two men with megaphones who walked around the periphery who would say, 'Now pitching for New York is so and so.' One of them was a man named Jack Lenz, who was a friend of my father's. He got me down to the dugout so I could meet Ruth and Gehrig."

Mara graduated from Loyola High School, a Jesuit institution across from the family's apartment at 83rd Street and Park Avenue. He then attended Fordham University, where he earned his degree in 1937. Jack Mara preceded him at Fordham, where he earned a law degree. But Wellington was only interested in joining his father with the Giants and did so immediately after graduation. Tim, Jack, and Wellington Mara formed the team's ruling triumvirate.

"It wasn't much of a structure, it was a just a way we did things that evolved," Wellington said. "Jack was the business manager, and I was the personnel director. I had the time to spend at training camp and practices. I was in close touch with [head coaches] Steve Owen and, later, Jim Lee Howell. We each ran our particular part of the business and then our father ran us. We'd talk things out and come to an agreement with one another on all the major issues.

"Jack was an attorney, and he was the conservative member of the family. During a typical discussion we would have about a player's contract, I'd be in favor of giving the player an amount of money. And Jack would say, 'Suppose we have a bad year?' And my father would say, 'How can we have a bad year?' Jack was pretty conservative, and my father and I both wanted to take a chance."

In those days the players were Mara's contemporaries, and he became close to many of them. Mara was good friends with Ward

Cuff, who played several positions for the Giants from 1937 to 1945. "It was a different era when you went on trips," Mara said. "When you went to Pittsburgh, instead of getting on a plane and flying for an hour, we'd get on a train, and I think it was a nine-hour trip. We played cards. I was part of a regular group that included Cuff; Orville Tuttle, who was a guard; Ed Danowski—there were maybe four or five of us. We played hearts, or pitch, which was a western game that I learned. We played from one year to the next. At the end of the year, you might have won five dollars or lost six. We were a pretty close unit, brought on by going on those long trips together."

Wellington Mara likes to say there are no ex-Giants, just old Giants. To him and his wife, Ann, anyone who wears Giants' blue is a member of the family for life. Of course Mara is closer to some members of the family than others. His dearest friend is Frank Gifford, whom he selected in the first round of the 1952 NFL draft. Mara and Gifford were each other's presenters at their Hall of Fame induction ceremonies. (Gifford was enshrined in 1977.) Gifford demonstrated his loyalty to the Mara family in 1965, when Jack Mara passed away. "He had just arrived in Hawaii on a long-delayed vacation that he really looked forward to," Wellington said. "When he got there, he heard that Jack had died. When he heard that, he got on the next plane back to New York. He said, 'If it weren't for Jack Mara, I never would have gotten to New York. I never would have gotten to Hawaii in the first place.' So we have a special bond. There's really nothing he would ask me to do that I wouldn't do." Mara, a horseracing fan his entire life, frequently plays, and often wins, a 1–6 daily double on his visits to the race-track. Gifford's number in his twelve-year Giants career was 16.

Mrs. Mara

Ann Mara is perhaps the most spirited member of the Mara family. "You can't talk about Mr. [Wellington] Mara without talking about his wife and his sons and daughters," said former quarterback Phil Simms. "To see them after victories and to see Mrs. Mara's face and knowing she was as competitive and enjoying the victories more than a lot of players, probably. Mrs. Mara complained to me after I retired about the team not winning the previous year. I said, 'Mrs. Mara, you went to the Super Bowl [recently].' She said, 'Phil, I expect to go to the Super Bowl every year.'"

The night before the Giants opened the 2003 season—September 6, 2003, to be exact—Gifford hosted a surprise party for Mara at Tavern on the Green in Central Park. More than eighty-five former—make that old—Giants from many different eras attended the party, which honored Mara for what was then a seventy-nine-year career with the Giants.

Mara didn't want to go to New York City that Saturday night. He awoke that day feeling a little under the weather. The Giants were facing the St. Louis Rams the following day, and Mara preferred to spend a quiet evening in his Westchester County home. But Gifford had implored him to go to Manhattan, saying his

Tim Mara (left), founder of the New York Giants, and Art Rooney, founder of the Pittsburgh Steelers. New York Giants

wife, Kathie Lee, was being honored at a dinner. And since Wellington and Ann Mara were the only family they had in the area, Frank said they simply had to attend. So Mara reluctantly put on a suit and headed to the famed restaurant.

Had Mara known it was he who was being honored, he would have remained home. Mara enjoys being in the spotlight about as much as he likes losing to the Washington Redskins. Gifford planned the surprise dinner for almost six months. Somehow, with the help of chairman and co-CEO Robert Tisch and others in the Giants' organization, the Mara family, and the most illustrious assemblage of former Giants to ever gather in one room, he pulled it off without Mara ever learning about it.

"He's done something for almost every Giant I've ever known," Gifford said. "And you've never heard him say anything about it. He just doesn't like being in the forefront. But he touched the lives of everyone who was there—including mine—and their families."

The gathering included Hall of Famers such as Lawrence Taylor, Y. A. Tittle, Sam Huff, and Rosie Brown, as well as relative unknowns like Billy Stribling, Bob Peviani, and Joe Wellborn, plus ten of Mara's eleven children and the vast majority of his then-thirty-seven grandchildren (he now has forty).

Had everyone spoken, those in attendance would have missed the game the following day. So the six Hall of Fame players in attendance addressed the crowd, offering tributes to Mara that were both heartfelt and humorous.

Huff told a story about his contract negotiations with Mara, who could be extremely tough in those situations. "We won the world championship my first year [1956], and I made rookie defensive player of the year at middle linebacker," Huff said. "I was making $7,500 at the time. When I was here, you dealt with Mr. Mara. And I wanted to deal with Jack, his brother. Wellington said, 'He deals with the offense, you have to deal with me.' I said, 'I want to deal with the same guy Charlie Conerly and Frank Gifford deal with.' He said, 'You're dealing with me.' I said, 'Yes, sir.' He said, 'Here's your raise—$500.' I said, 'Five hundred dollars!' He said, 'Sam, I think you're worth it.'"

The Duke

Somewhere along the way, Wellington Mara picked up the nickname "The Duke." For many years the NFL's official football was called The Duke, after Mara.

"It's from the name Wellington, the Duke of Wellington," Mara said. "My father said that the Duke of Wellington was a great fighting Irishman. I picked up the nickname when I was around the team and the players called me The Duke. It didn't bother me. I preferred it to Wellington.

"It was interesting, because most of the guys I went to school with called me Tim [his middle name]. Actually, I was christened Timothy Wellington Mara. But for some reason or another, I don't remember now why, it appears in the records as Wellington Timothy."

Taylor spoke movingly of his respect for and devotion to Mara. "Wellington has been there for me throughout the years," Taylor said. "I've had my problems. But while I played ball and after ball was over, he was always there. He never told me what to do. He'd say, 'You know what you have to do.' He'd never sit there and say, 'You can't do this' or 'You can't do that.' He was always ready to help me. I will always, always appreciate that."

"He's been as much my family as my family is," Gifford said. "He could be the perfect father, you'd be blessed to have him as a brother, and more than anything he's the best friend you can ever have. I think most of the guys [who attended the party] feel the same way. I talked to most of these guys individually, and each one of them had a story of something he had done for them. And these were not related to football. It had to do with their family, or they needed this or needed that, their kid needed a doctor."

Players from all generations of Giants have the same memories of Mara, because he has changed little over the years. He is a devout Catholic who attends Mass daily. Mara is humble and hardworking, still in the office regularly as he approaches his eighty-ninth birthday. And, as he has done since 1925, he attends most practices and games. At the former he used to watch while circling the field in a brisk walk, getting in his daily exercise as he watched the team prepare for its next game. Mara visits the locker room after every game, shaking hands with the coaches and players following a victory, offering words of encouragement after a defeat.

His game-day routine has changed little through the decades. "At home on a Sunday I go to eight o'clock Mass," he said. "I have a big breakfast when I get home, then leave for the stadium. I try to get to the stadium by ten o'clock. I walk through the dressing room, maybe check with the trainers about something—possibly an injured player, who's going to be available and who isn't. I like to walk through the dressing room so the people see that I'm there. I keep remembering what Michael Burke told me when he was running the Yankees. He had come from farming stock in Ireland, and he said his grandfather's favorite saying was, 'There's no fertilizer like the farmer's footsteps.'

"I'm not a glad-hander. I don't go up to a player and say, 'Have a good day.' I'm just there, that's all. I almost never go out on the field before the game. Once in a while if it's a special opponent we're playing, I'll go over and say hello—like to a [Bill] Parcells, maybe a John Fox, someone like that. But mostly I stay away. I don't believe in fraternizing on the day of the game."

Except with his family, whose members are with him on game day as they are every other day. Faith, family, and football are the marrow of Mara's life. Three of Wellington's sons are important members of the organization: John as executive vice president and chief operating officer; Chris as vice president of player evaluation; and Frank as director of promotions. Many of his grandsons are ball boys during training camp.

"The most fun I think was when my sons were very young and were first putting their toes in the water," Mara said. "It was fun seeing their reaction compared to what I remembered from when I was young. Now I have the same thing with the grandsons. There are all kinds of different reactions."

Not from Wellington Mara, whose core values and beliefs—and football rooting interests—have not changed for decades. "His sense of pride is tremendous," said quarterback Phil Simms, one of many former Giants who keep in touch with Mara. "I'll never forget this—we were coming out of training camp—it might have been 1986. Somebody got an interview with him. He didn't make a prediction. He said, 'I'm happy. The team was organized, the coach worked them hard, and they conducted themselves well.' I went, 'Wow, that's it.' I remember thinking that is so cool—that's the essence of what we are. And that's what makes him happy. Why? That's the way he wanted his team to act and be. But he also knew that's what's going to lead you to victory."

The man knows his stuff.

The Early Years

In the summer of 1925, Tim Mara knew absolutely nothing about football and had less interest in owning a pro football team. But he was a legal bookmaker, a promoter, and a renowned man about Manhattan who wasn't afraid to take chances and knew a good bet when he saw one. So on August 1, he agreed to pay $500 for the exclusive right to put a National Football League franchise in America's largest and busiest city.

Talk about a good return on his invest-ment. The Giants and the stadium that bears their name are today worth hundreds of millions of dollars. They are one of the most famous teams in professional sports, the flagship franchise of the NFL, an organization that proudly boasts championships and Hall of Famers and a season ticket waiting list approximately 20,000 names long.

Had Tim Mara, who was just thirty-eight years old when he bought the franchise, known all this was coming he would not have been so reluctant to invest in pro football, a game that was scarcely more popular than cricket with the nation's sporting public. It was not a football team that Mara wanted, but a boxer. Gene Tunney, who would one day outbox Jack Dempsey for the heavyweight championship, was Mara's favorite fighter. Mara, a friend to the city's politicians and bigwigs, as well as to the common citizens who legally bet with him at the racetrack, wanted a piece of Tunney.

He visited the office of his friend, Billy Gibson, who was also Tunney's manager. Gibson had no intention of selling Mara a stake in Tunney. But Mara didn't go away completely empty-handed. Also in Gibson's office that day were Joe Carr, a sports-writer from Ohio, and Harry A. March, a retired army surgeon who had just been named president of the five-year-old NFL. The men had been trying to convince Gibson to invest in the young league. With franchises in small cities like Duluth, Pottsville and, yes, Green Bay, league officials believed that a team in a large market such as New York was exactly what was needed to keep pro football alive. Gibson convinced Mara that a football franchise in the big city was a better long-term venture than Gene Tunney. Mara figured it was worth a $500 gamble.

"I figured even an empty store in New York City was worth $500," Mara later said.

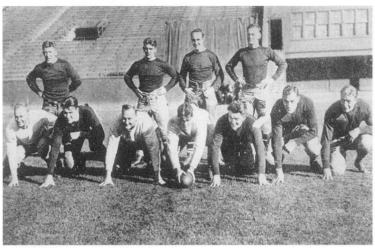

The inaugural Giants in 1925. New York Giants

Early on, it seemed an empty store might hold all the people who were interested in attending the games. Baseball and boxing were the popular spectator sports of the day. College football, with local favorites like NYU, Fordham, and Army, was also grabbing the public's attention. The NFL was mostly a curiosity.

But Mara was determined to make a go of it. Because it would play home games in the Polo Grounds, home of the baseball Giants, Mara named his team the New York Football Giants. In the early days of pro football, it was not unusual for teams to take the same name as their baseball cousins. At one time there were franchises named the New York Yankees, Cleveland Indians, Cincinnati Reds, and Detroit Tigers.

Although the Polo Grounds is best remembered for Bobby Thomson's pennant-winning home run in 1951 and Willie Mays's great catch with his back to home plate in the World Series three years later, Wellington Mara recalls it as a comfortable home where the Giants spent thirty-one seasons. "It was a better football stadium than it was a baseball stadium," Mara said. "There was a feeling of intimacy. I went to a number of games in Ebbets Field and felt the same thing there. There was the famous Section 5 Club. The section was way out in right-center field, and that was where you came up from downtown New York on the elevated train or the subway. You came in there and just sat there and that is how the club was formed. That carried over after the Polo Grounds was torn down, and there was a Section 5 Club in Yankee Stadium."

Tim Mara came up with $25,000 to pay players and a coach, purchase equipment, and take care of the rent, transportation, and other costs. March was named club secretary and placed in charge of assembling the team. He and Mara hired Robert Folwell, an experienced college coach, most recently at Navy, to be the Giants' first on-field leader.

Then, as now, star power was very important in New York. Mara and March decided to go after the biggest available football star, the legendary Jim Thorpe, who had played the previous season for the Rock Island Independents in Illinois. Thorpe was eager to come to New York, but he was then a thirty-seven-year-old player who was a mere shell of the athlete who had won both the decathlon and pentathlon in the 1912 Olympics. Mara hoped Thorpe would draw crowds and signed him to an unusual contract that called for the player to be paid $200 "per half game" since no one thought Thorpe could play a full sixty minutes.

The Giants took the field for the first time in a preseason game in early October in New Britain, Connecticut, against a team called Ducky Pond's All-Stars. No, they were not members of the NFL. Pond was a former star at Yale who would later become the head coach at his alma mater. The Giants won 26–0.

The NFL schedule was not as standardized as it is today. The Giants were slated to play their first two games on the road, then nine consecutive games in the Polo Grounds. They made the regular season debut on October 11, 1925, losing in Rhode Island to the Providence Steam Roller, 14–0. Six days later, they fell to the Frankford Yellow Jackets in Philadelphia, 5–3.

Both teams then took a train to New York for the Giants' home opener the following day (now that's a tough schedule). That Sunday, October 18, the Mara family attended Mass at Our Lady of Esperanza Roman Catholic Church on 156th Street and Riverside Drive. As the Maras, including nine-year-old Wellington, left the church, they stopped to chat with some of the other worshippers. Tim Mara told them, "I'm going to try to put pro football over in New York today."

To entice people to come out and see his new team, Mara offered tickets for as low as 50 cents. The top tickets were a whopping $2.75. Approximately 25,000 fans—about half of them admitted for free—attended the game, which the Giants lost 14–0. Thorpe played less than a half, was paid his $200, and was then released by Mara, who was at the game with his wife and sons, Jack and Wellington, who were already taking a keen interest in the team.

After losing their first three games, the Giants won seven in a row, five of them shutouts. But interest in the team among New Yorkers was lukewarm at best and, as the calendar turned to December, the Giants were mired in debt, perhaps as much as $40,000. One of Tim Mara's many influential friends was New

York's governor, Al Smith, who, according to Wellington, told his father, "Pro football will never amount to anything. Why don't you give it up?" Mara responded by saying, "The boys would run me right out of the house if I did."

But help was on the way in the form of Red Grange, the famed Galloping Ghost, who was as popular a sports figure as Babe Ruth or Jack Dempsey in 1925. Grange had played his final game for the University of Illinois on the Saturday before Thanksgiving and his first for the Chicago Bears just five days later. On December 6, the Bears were scheduled to visit the Polo Grounds.

Because the Army-Navy game had been played in the big stadium the previous week, thousands of extra seats were in place. That day pro football hit the big time in the big city. More than 70,000 fans jammed into the Polo Grounds, and thousands more watched from nearby Coogan's Bluff and the apartment buildings that surrounded the stadium.

The Bears proved to be too much for the Giants to handle that day, pulling away for a 19–7 victory. But the crowd showed little interest in the game's outcome or the fortunes of the home team. The attraction was Grange, who drew fans and nonfans alike, all lured in by curiosity. The crowd cheered when he played and appeared uninterested when he didn't. Grange's arrival at the Polo Grounds marked more than just an important football game. He became the first player in professional football to become bigger than the game and draw national attention. He was a star in every sense of the word; he not only paved the way for dozens of others to achieve the same kind of power and attention, but also allowed the owners in the young NFL to see what professional football could accomplish.

With the Bears clinging to a five-point lead in the fourth quarter, Grange intercepted a pass and returned it 35 yards for a touchdown. The Giants earned an estimated $40,000 that afternoon, effectively eliminating Tim Mara's losses. By the end of the season, he actually had made a small profit.

The game proved to be one of the most significant in Giants' history. On seeing the massive turnout for Grange, Mara dispelled any thoughts of selling the Giants and was encouraged to keep the team. Of course not everyone in the family was happy. "It was just a big game for me, and I was very disappointed that they beat us," Wellington Mara said.

Red Grange's visit to New York was one of the early turning points in pro football history. In 1925 college football dominated the late-autumn headlines. College football purists refused to acknowledge the NFL as a legitimate league, and the religious population was upset with playing of games on Sunday. Professional football was viewed by many as a negative influence on American athletics. Grange's decision to turn pro in 1925 was much more than simple decision. It was a heated debate, and everyone had an opinion.

"Nobody today realizes how hard the colleges fought pro ball," Grange once said. "The colleges were afraid that pro football would ruin college football. I'd have been more popular with some people if I'd joined Al Capone's mob in Chicago instead of the Bears."

A week after losing to Grange and Company, the Giants ended their first season in Chicago with a 9–0 victory over the Bears, giving them an 8–4 record. They continued to struggle financially through the first decade but managed to win their first title in only their third season, going 11–1–1 in 1927. With the fall of the stock market and the Great Depression that followed, the 1930s were not off to a great start. Tim Mara suffered substantial losses during the crash, which threatened the existence of the Giants. With that in mind, in 1930, Tim Mara handed control of the franchise over to Jack, who was then twenty-two, and Wellington, who at just fourteen was the youngest owner of a football team.

There were many anxious moments for NFL owners in those days. "We would wake up Sunday morning looking at the weather right away, because the weather controlled your game," Wellington said. "My father used to buy rain insurance. As I recall, it had to rain one-eighth of an inch between 12:00 and 2:00 P.M. Sunday afternoon to collect. He never collected. We had a lot of rain, but he never collected."

Despite the team's sometimes shaky finances, it succeeded on the field. Two years after winning their first championship, the Giants were 13–1–1, and the following season they finished 13–4. In 1933 the NFL split into two divisions. The Giants easily won the Eastern Division with an 11–3 record, but they lost the first-ever league title game to the Bears, 23–17.

They got their revenge the next season in one of the most famous football games ever played—the "Sneakers Game."

In 1934 the Giants again finished atop their division, this time with an 8–5 record. On December 9 they hosted their old nemesis, Chicago, in the NFL Championship Game. A month earlier, the Bears had crushed the Giants 27–7 in Chicago on their way to a 13–0 finish. The Bears expected to cap their perfect season by winning another title in the Polo Grounds.

The weather in New York was ghastly that afternoon. The temperature was nine degrees and the field was covered with a sheet of ice, making it more suitable for hockey than football. The protective tarp on the field did little, seeing that it froze to the ground. The Giants wondered how they would ever stop Chicago's Bronko Nagurski, the strongest running back of his day. The 35,059 fans who braved the elements saw Chicago physically dominate the Giants while taking a 10–3 halftime lead. Nagurski scored the Bears' touchdown, on a 1-yard run. Both teams were slipping and sliding around the field. Then Abe Cohen, a 5' 2", 140-pound tailor, became the unlikeliest hero in NFL history.

Here's how: Ray Flaherty, an end who had played at Gonzaga College in Washington State, recalled a game against Montana in which his team had enjoyed superior traction by wearing basketball sneakers. At breakfast the morning of the game, he suggested to legendary coach Steve Owen that the Giants do the same. Owen, eager to try anything to slow down Nagurski and the Bears, called the two big sporting goods stores then in New York, A. G. Spalding and Alex Taylor. Both stores were closed. That's when Cohen got his chance to step into the spotlight, a nice place to be on a frigid day.

Cohen had worked for Chick Meehan, a coach at Manhattan College, who was the first to put satin pants on his football team. Cohen was the tailor who made sure the pants fit properly. "Chick was a showman," Wellington Mara said. "Those pants were very flashy looking."

The Giants weren't looking for gaudy pants. They needed a shoe that would enable them to slip past the powerful Bears on the frozen field of the Polo Grounds. Owen sent Cohen over to Manhattan College, where he had a key to the equipment room, and asked him to gather up as many pairs of sneakers as he could find.

"Abe Cohen, I don't know if he volunteered or was drafted," Mara said. "I think it was not until the team got to the Polo Grounds that that suggestion came on. He said, 'I'll go up to Manhattan and get the basketball team's shoes. And he got in a cab and went up there and broke into this locker room. He came back with about ten pairs of sneakers at halftime. Some of the players didn't want to put them on. But a couple of players put them on and they worked, so everyone put them on. And the story was that when the Bears went over to their sideline they said to George Halas, 'Coach, Coach, they're wearing basketball shoes.' And Halas said, 'Then step on their toes.'"

The Polo Grounds, the Giants' home from 1925 to 1955. New York Giants

If You Can't Beat 'em, Join 'em

Wellington Mara adds a postscript to the story of the Sneakers Game:

"In those days you had barnstorming trips after the season was over, and the next week the Bears played an exhibition game in Philadelphia," Mara said. "Steve Owen and I took the train down to see the game. We went into the Bears' dressing room—I guess we wanted to gloat a little bit—and there were all these basketball shoes. They had bought a whole set of basketball shoes.

"[George] Halas said to us, 'I'll never get caught like that again.'"

Chicago stretched its lead to 13–3 by the end of the third period. But the Giants, benefiting from their improved traction, outscored the Bears 27–0 in the fourth quarter. Ed Danowski threw a 28-yard touchdown pass to Mal Frankian and scored on a 9-yard run, while Ken Strong stepped through the skidding and sliding Bears on scoring runs of 42 and 11 yards. The final score was 30–13, Giants.

"I think the sneakers gave them an edge in that last half, for they were able to cut back when they were running with the ball and we couldn't cut with them," said Nagurski, who complimented his opponents. "We feel that everyone has to lose some time, but this is a pretty hard time to start. The Giants, though, were a fine ball team, and their comeback in that second half was the greatest ever staged against us."

Manhattan basketball coach Neil Cohalan said, "I'm glad to hear our basketball shoes did the Giants some good. The question now is, did the Giants do our basketball shoes any good?"

For Tim Mara, the Sneakers Game was one of the sweetest victories he ever witnessed. "I never was so pleased with anything in all my life," he said. "In all the other contests with the Bears, I always have hoped the whistle would blow and end the game. [In that game,] I was hoping it would last for a couple of hours."

The Giants returned to the title game the following season, but they lost to the Detroit Lions, 26–7. They won their second championship game in 1938, 23–17, against Green Bay, but lost to the Packers the following year, 27–0.

Mara has been close to every team the Giants have ever fielded. Do any stand out to him?

"I think the 1938 team does, because they were my contemporaries," he said. "In 1937 out of a twenty-five-man squad, I think we had seventeen rookies. They obviously had all gotten out of school the same time I got out in '37. I saw them come along and develop into a really good team in '38. Quite a few of the players from that team fought in World War II. How far they might have gone if the war hadn't come along, I don't know.

"You can't rate teams of one era against teams of another era. What you have to do is see how they compare with the teams of their own era. I think that team had an edge in depth and youth and they were really very good. I don't like the word *dynasty*, but they won for many years."

The Giants had many great players in that era, including Hall of Famers Mel Hein, Tuffy Leemans, and Strong. But Mara's fondest memories are reserved for one of his fellow players in those long-ago card games. "Maybe my favorite player was Ward Cuff, because he was my roommate," Mara said. "He was a cornerback and wingback in those days. He was also our place-kicker and kickoff man—a very aggressive player. He was an all-around athlete. He was a championship javelin thrower at Marquette."

Despite the efforts of Cuff and others, the Giants lost championship games in 1941 (37–9 to the Bears), 1944 (14–7 to the Packers), and 1946 (24–14 to the Bears). They would not win another title until 1956, one of the most memorable and magical seasons in the Giants' illustrious history.

1956

The year 1956 was important and exciting in the United States and around the world. Dwight D. Eisenhower was reelected president, defeating Adlai Stevenson for the second time. Soviet troops suppressed a popular uprising against the Communist regime in Hungary, and Congress approved the Highway Act, which allowed for construction of the U.S. interstate highway system. Elvis's "Heartbreak Hotel" topped the *Billboard* charts, *Around the World in Eighty Days* received the Academy Award as best picture, and America's favorite television show was *I Love Lucy*.

Also, 1956 may have been the most significant year in Giants history. After more than three decades in the Polo Grounds, they crossed the Harlem River and began playing their home games in Yankee Stadium. Andy Robustelli was obtained in a trade, and Sam Huff arrived via the draft. Frank Gifford was the NFL's player of the year, and Rosie Brown the lineman of the year. (All four players would one day be enshrined in the Pro Football Hall of Fame.) The Giants won the league championship by again crushing the Bears after donning sneakers on a frigid, slippery day, just as they had done twenty-two years before. Although they would play in five title games in eight years, they would not win another championship for thirty years. It was also the year New York began to embrace the Giants as favorite sons.

The move to Yankee Stadium, which enabled the Giants to depart an aging, crumbling stadium, was precipitated by an offer the Mara family received to sell the Giants. "What happened was that Bert Bell, who was the commissioner at the time, called up my father and told him that 'two Texas oilmen' had offered a million dollars for the Giants," Wellington Mara said. "We never did find out who it was. We thought it might have been Clint Murchison [the first owner of the Dallas Cowboys], but we didn't know. That was all of the money in the world. But the offer was only good if we would move the team to Yankee Stadium. We lived up in Riverdale and my brother Jack lived there. My father came up on a Sunday morning. The three of us sat down and my father said, 'If our team is worth a million dollars in Yankee Stadium, and nothing in the Polo Grounds, we had better move to Yankee Stadium.' And we moved because of that."

It was not quite as simple as that. Tim Mara and Yankees owner Dan Topping did not get along. Dan Topping had owned the football Yankees of the rival All-America Conference from 1946 to 1949, and Mara didn't appreciate the competition for New York's football public. Jack Mara, who was an attorney, was able to work out a deal with Topping allowing the Giants to play in Yankee Stadium.

It was fortunate that he did. After the 1957 baseball season, the Giants and Dodgers left New York for San Francisco and Los Angeles, respectively. "At that time we had no suspicion that the baseball Giants and the Dodgers were getting ready to move to San Francisco and Los Angeles," Wellington Mara said. "We could have been left with a real white elephant on our hands because the Polo Grounds was crumbling and required a great deal of maintenance. We would have been the only team left there. It would have been a real disaster for us. So it was a great move."

The players loved it. Oh, they weren't thrilled about having to wait until the Yankees concluded their season before they could line the field, particularly since the baseball team was a regular participant in the World Series. That forced the Giants to play almost all of their preseason games and first three regular games on the road each year, plus practice at Fordham University. But Yankee Stadium was the most famous sports venue in the world. And they got to use the same locker room and field as the Yankees, the most successful and celebrated sports franchise in

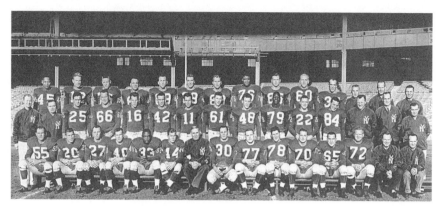

The 1956 NFL Champion Giants. New York Giants

America. Defensive back Dick Nolan remembers several players fooling around before practice, trying to hit baseballs with their helmets and shoulder pads on.

"Playing in Yankee Stadium was like playing in the Hall of Fame," Huff said. "It was overwhelming to me to come to New York [from West Virginia] and be part of the whole scene. When you think of Yankee Stadium, you think of Babe Ruth, you think of Lou Gehrig, you think of Joe DiMaggio. At that time it was just so great. Mickey Mantle, he was an interesting person. And then there was Roger Maris and Whitey Ford and Yogi Berra. That was such a great time, because all of us knew each other. We went to a place called Toots Shor's [a famed sports saloon in Manhattan]. The great thing about Toots Shor is he never charged us for anything. He loved me because I was part of the defense. He always gave me the booth up front right next to the bar, because he liked to sit at the bar. He'd say, 'If Gifford comes in, he's going to the back, because he's part of the offense.'" (Gifford disputes that, saying he was also one of Shor's favorites.)

"Yankee Stadium wasn't a lot better than the Polo Grounds, but it had an aura about it," Gifford said. "I remember the first time I walked in there, like a lot of people, I went out to center field to look at the monuments. I had Mantle's locker. I had actually seen Mickey when I was at USC. The football field we had spring practice on was parallel to the third-base line of the baseball field. One day in spring practice, a ball came over the fence. It had never happened before. It was way back—there was a gap between that and the spring practice field. We got back to the locker room and someone said, 'Some kid named Mickey Mantle hit that ball.' It was the first time I ever heard his name. Five years later we had the same home."

When the Giants played in Yankee Stadium, Wellington Mara and Ken Kavanaugh, an assistant coach for sixteen seasons and later a scout for the team, would sit in the press box and take photographs of the opposing team's offensive and defensive formations with an instant camera. They'd stuff the pictures inside a sock weighted with football cleats, then toss them down to the Giants bench, where they were studied by the players and coaches.

Unlike today, when most of the Giants are scattered around northern New Jersey, many of the 1956 Giants lived, as did several Yankees, in the Concourse Plaza Hotel. It was close enough to the stadium that they could walk, en masse, to practice. After games they would often gather for parties, most often in Gifford's apartment, but sometimes in Charlie Conerly's or Kyle Rote's.

"A lot of us lived at the Concourse Plaza," Sam Huff said. "Plus the baseball team lived there. And a lot of times, the visiting teams stayed at the Concourse Plaza. It was only a block to Yankee Stadium. It's almost like you fall out of bed and roll down a hill and you're in Yankee Stadium. It was very convenient."

"It was a magic time to be in New York," said Pat Summerall, a reserve on offense and defense, as well as the team's kicker. "More than any other team, I think, we were the darlings of New York. I don't remember ever paying for a meal. Everywhere you went, people wanted to be with you. They wanted to socialize with you, hang around. We spent a lot of Sunday nights at P. J. Clark's [another popular bar]. It was a great time; the best time, certainly of the years that I have been in football. It was the most fun time of my life. We all lived up at the Concourse Plaza and we'd walk to practice together. After practice was over, we'd walk back and stop and have a beer together. It was a very close-knit group. We hung together all of the time."

As word spread about these postgame parties, prominent people from other walks of life began attending. One of them was Richard Nixon, an avid Giants fan who just happened to be the vice president of the United States. "We had a lot of famous people up there," Gifford said. "Richard Nixon came up to my apartment a couple of times. I'd met him at a game in Washington when he came down to the field and he introduced himself. His wife Pat had gone to USC. And he was a big football fan. I have about twenty handwritten letters from him. After almost anything that would happen to me after that time, he would write me a letter."

On the field the 1956 Giants were coached by Jim Lee Howell, who had succeeded Hall of Famer Steve Owen two years earlier. Howell's top assistants were Vince Lombardi on offense and Tom Landry on defense, two brilliant strategists who would later win multiple championships as head coaches in Green Bay and

Memorable Guy

In 1971 Frank Gifford became the play-by-play announcer on ABC's *Monday Night Football* telecasts. His first game was to be the annual Hall of Fame game from Canton, Ohio, which was played on a Sunday afternoon. Roone Arledge, then the head of ABC Sports, called Gifford to tell him that Richard Nixon, who was then president, was making a speech in nearby Cleveland the day before the game. Arledge asked Gifford to call the White House to see if Nixon would attend the game.

"He was going to make his historic trip to China, which ultimately turned the whole world around," Gifford said. "I called and said I was Frank Gifford, an acquaintance of the president, and I left a message asking if he could call back. Sure enough, he called back and said, 'I'm going to try to be there. I've always wanted to visit the Hall of Fame.' He put somebody else on the line, and I put him together with ABC's office. Sure enough, he made the speech in Cleveland, then came to the Hall of Fame. It was my first game with ABC and I was rehearsing. Roone was waiting for Nixon in the rotunda of the Hall of Fame. This was the president of the United States, literally on his way to China to change the world. He told Roone, 'I think Frank will remember me, I used to go to his apartment in New York.'"

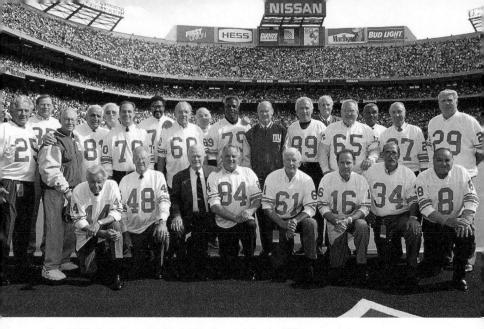

The 1956 champions at a Giants Stadium reunion in 1996.

Dallas, respectively, on their way to the Hall of Fame.

The star-studded cast of players included seven Pro Bowlers in Gifford, Conerly, Robustelli, Rosie Brown, Rosey Grier, Kyle Rote, and Emlen Tunnell. Huff was in his rookie season in a Hall of Fame career. Outstanding players such as Alex Webster, Mel Triplett, and Dick Modzelewski were also vital contributors on that team.

"Not only were they great players and great athletes, they were all kind of bright," Summerall said. "And I think we won a lot of games because we were just smarter than the other people. I know that was the case. That was one of the things that I thought when I first got there [in a trade] from the Cardinals, that it was a bunch of bright guys."

"I think it was the best team for me to play on, because I was the total focal point of the offense," said Gifford, who led the team in rushing (819 yards), receiving (51 catches), and scoring (65 points). Lombardi believed in that; Paul Hornung became me up in Green Bay. We might have had better personnel in 1962 and '63, but it's arguable that '56 was the best team I ever played on. The defense was emerging. Our offense was not swift, but it was good. We ran the ball well with Webster, Triplett, and me. We controlled the ball. The defense didn't get all the acclaim it would later, because we moved the ball. We were good."

The Giants held training camp that year at St. Michael's College in Winooski, Vermont. After playing a preseason schedule that took them to Boston, Green Bay, Seattle, Portland, New York, and Memphis, they opened the regular season on September 30 with a 38–21 victory in San Francisco. After losing to the Cardinals in Chicago, the Giants won their next five games: at Cleveland, home against Pittsburgh and Philadelphia, at Pittsburgh, and in Yankee Stadium against the Cards. On November 18 they suffered their worst defeat of the season, 33–7, at Washington. The following week they tied the Bears in the Bronx, 17–17. They won a home game against the Redskins, lost one to the Browns, then concluded the season with a 21–7 triumph in Philadelphia.

As the season wore on, the Giants began to captivate New York as they never had before. It was an exciting, close-knit team that scored a conference-best 264 points. "We all got along so well," Webster later recalled. "Most of the players lived in the Concourse Plaza, and we spent a lot of time together off the field.

On the field there was a feeling of unselfishness, of doing what was best for the team. We knitted together as the year went on and got better and better."

Defensively, Landry eschewed the five-man line then in vogue and used Huff as a middle linebacker in a 4–3 defense. During the five-game winning streak, the Giants allowed only 46 points, prompting a new chant to echo from the stadium stands: "Dee-fense, Dee-fense." The defense was so good, and so popular, the Giants began to introduce the defense prior to games instead of the offense. "At that time they never introduced the defensive units, never ever," Huff said. "We were the first defensive unit to be introduced."

The Giants' 8–3–1 record was good enough to win the Eastern Conference and host the NFL Championship Game in Yankee Stadium. Their opponents were the Bears, whom they faced for the fifth time with the league title on the line. Chicago had won in 1933, 1941, and 1946. The Giants' only championship game victory over their ancient rivals was in the Sneakers Game in 1934. Chicago, which had won the Western Conference with a 9–2–1 record, had both the NFL's leading rusher in Rick Casares (1,126 yards) and leading passer in Ed Brown (1,667 yards). Perhaps for that reason, the Bears were installed as a three-point favorite.

On December 30, 1956, New York had, as Huff recalls, "cold, bitter, nasty weather." In similar conditions twenty-two years earlier, several Giants had donned sneakers for the second half of their championship game against the Bears and took advantage of their superior footing by outscoring Chicago, 27–0, in the fourth quarter of a 34–13 victory. In the week leading up to the 1956 game, Wellington Mara saw how frozen the field was and suggested to Howell that the Giants again wear sneakers. Howell conducted a test in which rookie back Gene Filipski ran around the field in sneakers, while defensive back Ed Hughes did the same in cleats. Filipski glided effortlessly, while Hughes slipped and spilled. Mara and Howell approached Robustelli, who owned a sporting goods store, and asked him to provide the team with rubber-soled shoes. Four dozen pairs arrived in time for the game.

This time, the Giants didn't wait to put them on. They emerged from the dugout to start the game wearing basketball shoes. The Bears, who were caught by surprise in the Polo Grounds in 1934, were ready for the slick conditions; many of their players wore sneakers as well. But the footwear made no difference. The Giants jumped out to leads of 13–0 after the first period and 34–7 at halftime on their way to a resounding 47–7 triumph.

"The Bears were supposed to be the roughest team in football," Gifford said. "As we quickly discovered, however, they had no idea what we were up to. Our offense and defense just kept outsmarting them, doing things they had never seen before and that are done all the time today. We were playing really well. At the end of the season, we had some really solid games against some tough teams. Charlie was throwing the ball well. At that point I was our leading receiver and leading rusher. They'd flank me out in passing situations, and I ran the ball on short yardage. Triplett had a big game—we all did. The sneakers helped a lot."

Don Heinrich started at quarterback for the Giants, who took possession following the opening kick on the Chicago 39 yard line, thanks to a 53-yard return by Filipski. Gifford's 22-yard reception set up Triplett's 17-yard touchdown run up the middle that gave the Giants an early 7–0 lead.

"I think one of the key plays of that game was we had a third and 12 or 13 on the first series, and I ran an out on J. C. Caroline," Gifford said. "I made a move to the inside and broke it out, and he fell right on his ass. We got the first down and went on to score. He was their number-one defensive back, and not only did he not cover me, he fell on his ass. And we got a key first down and they thought, 'Holy mackerel, we're in trouble.'"

If the Bears thought they had problems after the Giants' first possession, that feeling surely intensified after their very first offensive snap. Brown and Casares muffed a handoff, causing a fumble that Robustelli recovered at Chicago's 15 yard line. That led to Ben Agajanian's 17-yard field goal and a 10–0 lead. (Agajanian had lost all the toes on his kicking foot in an industrial accident as a young man.)

On the Bears' next series, Jimmy Patton intercepted Brown's pass and returned it to the Chicago 36 yard line. Agajanian then kicked his longest field goal of the season, a 43-yarder, for a 13-point lead.

The second period also belonged to the home team. Conerly's 22-yard pass to Webster set up the running back's 3-yard touchdown run. The Giants again stopped Chicago, but then they made a rare mistake as Tunnel fumbled a punt and John Melakis recovered for the Bears at the Giants 25. The turnover led to Casares's 9-yard scoring run up the middle. George Blanda kicked the extra point, and it was 20–7 with eight minutes left in the half.

Good times were short-lived for the Bears. Conerly's 50-yard pass to Webster put the Giants on Chicago's 22 yard line. Four plays later, Webster bulled into the end zone from a yard out. On Chicago's next possession, Grier sacked Brown on the 1 yard line, forcing Brown to punt from the end zone. The kick was blocked by Ray Beck, and Henry Moore, a rookie from Arkansas, recovered it in the end zone to make it 34–7.

The second half was academic. Conerly threw touchdown passes of 9 yards to Rote in the third quarter and 14 yards to Gifford in the fourth to close the scoring. When the gun sounded, the Giants had won their first championship in eighteen years.

"I had such confidence in our team," Mara said. "But I had to be surprised at that [the margin of victory] because the Bears were a really good team." Gifford said, "It was one of those games that, played on a different day in a different stadium, it could have gone the other way. But I think we were better than they were."

The Greatest Game Ever Played

In 1957 running back Jimmy Brown joined the Cleveland Browns as the team's first-round draft choice. The Giants and Browns were then engaged in one of the most heated rivalries in the NFL, their twice-yearly skirmishes among the most fiercely competitive games in the league. Brown's arrival added heat to an already boiling pot, particularly because it pitted him against the

Giants ferocious middle linebacker, Sam Huff. Huff and Brown had faced each other in college, when the former was at West Virginia University and Brown was an All-American at Syracuse. In the pros the classic one-on-one battles between these two future Hall of Famers became legendary.

"My second year, along came Jim Brown," Huff said. "When Tom Landry gave a scouting report to the defense, he said, 'This guy is perhaps the greatest player that you'll ever see.' I knew who he was. In college he was a junior and I was a senior when I hit him so hard I knocked myself out. He was something. He could run over people. Tom said, 'Well, he's your man. It's up to you to stop him.' Jim Brown was the greatest football player that's ever played, that's ever touched a football."

Cleveland twice beat the Giants in Brown's rookie season, taking the season opener 6–3, then winning the season finale in Yankee Stadium, 34–28. Those two games were the difference in the Eastern Conference race, which the Browns won by two and one half games over the Giants. But Cleveland's crushing 59–14 loss to the Detroit Lions in the NFL Championship Game convinced the Giants that they were superior to their intense rivals.

The Giants were determined to prove that when the 1958 season opened. After splitting their first four games, they won three in a row, including a 21–17 decision in Cleveland. But when they met on December 14—again, in the season finale—the Browns held a one-game lead in the conference race. That meeting kicked off perhaps the most memorable and remarkable three-week stretch in Giants history.

Thanks to an improbable field goal by Pat Summerall that was believed to be 49 yards long, the Giants won 13–10 forging a tie at the top of the conference. The following week the Browns returned to Giants Stadium for an Eastern Conference playoff game. The Giants won that one 10–0. Then, on December 28 the Giants hosted the Baltimore Colts in the NFL Championship Game. In the first overtime game in league history, the Colts earned a 23–17 triumph on Alan Ameche's 1-yard run at 8:15 of sudden death. Today, almost a half-century later, it is still called "the Greatest Game Ever Played."

"That was a great run," Frank Gifford said of the three-week stretch.

It began with a scintillating victory against their archrivals. Jim Brown's 65-yard touchdown run on the game's first play from scrimmage had helped give the Browns a 10–3 lead through three quarters. The swirling snow that had enveloped the stadium all afternoon began to intensify as the teams headed for the final act. The Giants tied the score on an option play in which Gifford threw a 7-yard touchdown pass to Bob Schnelker. But a tie did the Giants no good; they needed a victory to force a playoff.

Prior to that season, Mara, believing he needed a kicker, sent Dick Nolan and Bobby Joe Conrad to the Bears for Summerall and running back Linden Crow. It proved to be a providential trade for the Giants when the season hung in the balance.

Late in the fourth quarter, Summerall, who had kicked a 46-yard field goal for the Giants' first points, misfired on a 31-yard attempt that would have put them ahead for the first time. Several Giants players approached Summerall to tell him he'd get another shot. But he wasn't as certain. Less than five minutes remained, and Cleveland had a chance to run out the clock. But the Browns failed, giving the Giants a last chance by fumbling away the football. The Giants offense could only advance to Cleveland's 42, and facing a fourth down in the heavy snow, Coach Jim Lee Howell made the shocking decision to send Summerall on the field for another field-goal try. This time, incredibly, the kick sailed through the uprights to give the Giants a 13–10 victory.

The field goal went into the record books as a 49-yarder, but to this day no one is certain how far it traveled. Not that anyone on the Giants cared. All that mattered was that the Giants had vanquished their foe and remained in the running for a championship.

Wellington Mara, who has seen it all in his eighty-one years with the franchise, calls Summerall's field goal the biggest play in Giants history. Two photos of the ball clearing the goal posts are among the many pictures hanging in his office. "It is the biggest because of the circumstances of the play, and because the result of it put us in the [conference] championship," Mara said. "We never did find out how far it was. I always thought it was further than 49. I remember very well I was up in the box with [assistant coach Ken] Kavanaugh and I forget who else. When Summerall was sent on the field, we all second-guessed the decision. We thought he couldn't kick it that far."

They weren't alone in their thinking. Vince Lombardi, the offensive assistant, tried to talk Howell out of deploying Summerall. "When Jim Lee had called for the field goal that we ultimately made, not too many people were in favor of that," Summerall said. "When I got to the huddle, Charlie Conerly, who was the quarterback and the holder, said, 'What the hell are you doing in here?' I couldn't believe he asked me to do that. The field was in horrible shape, and I had never made a kick that long."

His longest field goal of the season was the 46-yarder he had kicked earlier in the game. Now Summerall was being asked to try an even longer kick, under incredible pressure, in abominable conditions. Summerall knew he was a long way from the goal line. He figured he'd kick the ball as hard as he could and hope for the best.

"I don't know how long it was," he said. "Kyle Rote said that it was back at the 50. There was no way to tell because all of the lines were obliterated by the snow. They were not marked like they are today. And it was in mud and dirt, anyway. I remember I knew I had hit it solidly. I knew that. And the wind and the snow and the mist, like it was at Yankee Stadium, if you hit the ball solidly and hit it up close to the center like you have to, to get it that far, it behaves like a knuckleball. I remember watching as it got closer to the goal post; it was breaking back and forth like a knuckler. And I wasn't sure it was going to go in; I knew it was far enough, but I wasn't sure it was going to go in."

When it did, with a little more than two minutes remaining, pandemonium raged on the field, on the sideline, and in the stands. After being hugged and slapped on the back by his teammates who had shared the huddle, Summerall made his way over to the sideline. One of the first men to greet him was Lombardi. "He grabbed me, and I thought he was going to say, 'Great kick' or something of a congratulatory nature," Summerall said. "But he said, 'You know, you SOB, you can't kick it that far.'"

"I was on the field-goal team," Huff said. "There wasn't any doubt in my mind he could make it. The ball went clear over the crossbar, I think into the stands. He really drilled it."

Summerall's field goal for the ages left the two teams tied with 9–3 records. The coin toss to determine who would host the

Eastern Conference playoff game was won by the Giants, so the Browns invaded Yankee Stadium for the second week in a row on December 21. This time, the game was not nearly as dramatic. The Giants' defense, determined to stop the hard-rushing Brown, held him to a career-low 8 yards on 7 carries before a vicious hit by Huff knocked him out of the game.

The Giants scored the only points they needed in the first quarter on an unorthodox play sent in by Lombardi. From Cleveland's 19 yard line, Conerly, who was then thirty-seven years old, took the snap and handed the ball to Alex Webster, who then gave the ball to Gifford. The star running back ran to the 8, where he lateraled the ball back to Conerly as he was about to be tackled. Conerly covered the remaining ground for a touchdown. Summerall completed the scoring with a 26-yard field goal in the second period.

The two-week sweep of their archrivals put the Giants into the NFL Championship Game against the Colts. The thrilling game proved to be a defining moment in the history of the NFL. Because it featured so many high-profile stars (Gifford, Huff, Johnny Unitas, and Gino Marchetti, to name four Hall of Famers) and because of its breathtaking conclusion, that game, more than any other event, raised the profile and popularity of pro football and helped elevate the NFL into the forefront of the nation's sports consciousness.

"We didn't know it at the time, but it was the beginning for us," the late Pete Rozelle would tell a reporter years later, when he was NFL commissioner. "From that game forward, our fan base grew and grew. We owe both franchises a huge debt."

Of course the Giants considered none of those far-reaching implications when they took the field that frigid afternoon in the

Hall of Famer Frank Gifford,
who played for the Giants from
1952 to 1964. *New York Giants*

Bronx. Their simple goal was to win a second championship in three years. What they got instead was searing disappointment and leading roles in a historic drama.

No one was more upset than Gifford. He fumbled the ball away twice in the second period, turnovers the Colts turned into touchdowns to take a 14–3 lead. "My fumbles are the reason it's called 'the Greatest Game Ever Played,'" Gifford said. "If I hadn't fumbled the ball—once going in for a touchdown and once going out—and they scored on both of them, we wouldn't even be talking about that as the greatest game ever played."

The Colts weren't the greatest team the Giants had ever faced, but they were good. Baltimore had won the Western Conference with a 9–3 record that included a 24–21 loss to the Giants on November 9. But the Colts were the NFL's highest-scoring team, averaging 31.8 points per game, and their defense was among the league's best. And they had rested the previous Sunday, while the Giants skirmished with the Browns.

Summerall's 36-yard field goal late in the first quarter gave the Giants a 3–0 lead. On the first play of the second period, Gifford caught a pass from Conerly, but he fumbled and the ball was recovered by Gene "Big Daddy" Lipscomb. Five plays later Ameche scored from 2 yards out for the Colts first lead.

The Giants next possession stalled, but Don Chandler's punt was fumbled by Baltimore's Jackie Simpson and recovered by Melwood Guy on Baltimore's 10 yard line. But Gifford coughed up the ball again on the very next play. Don Joyce recovered on the 14, launching a 14-play, 86-yard drive that ended with Unitas throwing a 15-yard touchdown pass to Raymond Berry. The Colts took their 14–3 lead into the halftime locker room.

Baltimore had a chance to increase its lead in the third period after picking up a first down at the Giants 3 yard line. But the Giants defense made a terrific stand, capped when linebacker Cliff Livingston dumped Ameche for a 2-yard loss to the 5 yard line on fourth down. The Giants then drove the length of the field, with help, ironically, from another fumble. Conerly threw a long pass to Kyle Rote, who lost the ball at the Colt 25 yard line. Webster scooped it up and ran to the 1. Two plays later Triplett scored to make it 14–10.

With the momentum in their favor, the Giants kept attacking. On the first play of the fourth quarter, Conerly threw a 46-yard pass to Bob Schnelker, giving the Giants a first down at Baltimore's 15. On the next play, Gifford caught a pass near the right sideline, evaded two tacklers and stepped into the end zone. The Giants were back on top 17–14.

The Greatest Game Ever Played was not played particularly well. As the fourth quarter progressed, the Colts muffed a field-goal attempt, Giants back Phil King lost a fumble that was recovered by Ordell Brase, and the Colts failed to capitalize on the takeaway and were forced to punt.

The Giants had a chance to effectively clinch the game when they faced a third and four at their own 40 with just over two minutes remaining. Because they believed the Colts expected a pass, the Giants pitched the ball to Gifford, who ran to his right, cut inside Marchetti, the great defensive end, and appeared to pick up the critical first down. Then things got complicated.

Lipscomb's 290-pound body fell on Marchetti's leg, breaking it. As Marchetti screamed in agony, chaos ensued, and the officials failed to mark the ball. When it was finally placed down, it was well short of the first-down marker. All these years later, Gifford is convinced he gained the necessary yardage.

"There's no question in my mind, even this far removed from it," Gifford said. "There wasn't any question at the time. Marchetti broke his leg and was screaming like a panther at the bottom of the pile, and the official didn't pay any attention to where he marked the ball. I didn't even look over at the yard markers. I had played long enough in high school, college, and the pros to know I had made the first down. I didn't have to see it. But when they untangled everybody and marked the ball, it was a couple inches short.

"We [the players] all wanted to go for it [on fourth down]. And Lombardi wanted to go for it. Howell didn't want to go for it. It was arguable either way. I would have gone for it had I been coaching, just for the sheer awareness that we were a beat-up offensive team. We didn't have anything left, Charlie in particular. We left everything out there. It just happened that Gino Marchetti broke his leg. You can't sit around and gripe your whole life about something like that. If I don't fumble the ball, it's not even a contest."

Howell ordered Don Chandler to punt, and Baltimore took possession at the 14 yard line with only two minutes remaining. When Unitas threw two incompletions, the Giants seemed on the verge of icing the game. But the twenty-five-year-old quarterback kept the Colts alive by completing an 11-yard pass to Lenny Moore. After another incompletion, the famed duo of Unitas and Berry hooked up on three consecutive passes covering 62 yards. With just 7 seconds remaining, Steve Myrha kicked a 20-yard field goal to tie the score at 17–17.

"Johnny Unitas moved that ball against probably what was the best defense maybe that's ever been in the National Football

League—against us, down the field to tie the game," Huff said. "He made the plays when he had to make them."

A captivated nation of football fans watched the spectacle on television, anxious to see what would happen next. (But they weren't watching in New York, where the game was blacked out.) They didn't know it, but many of the players on their screens were utterly confused about what to do after Myrha's field goal.

"Nobody knew what was going to happen," Summerall said. "Nobody knew what we were supposed to do. I asked Don Heinrich, the backup quarterback, 'What happens now?' He said, 'I don't have any idea.' It seemed we waited for an eternity, I know it was more than three minutes before we started to play again. We went back out for another coin toss, obviously. There was just confusion on the bench—nobody knew what was going on."

"Nobody had ever talked about sudden death in a football game," Huff said. "We finished the game 17–17, and we're standing on the sideline trying to figure out how much money we get. Because you tied and so you figured you got half the money, which in those days wasn't very much money anyway. So over comes the referee and he said, 'Okay, here's the deal.' We're kind of all around him, 'What do you mean deal?' 'Here's the deal—in three minutes we're going to flip the coin again, and first team that scores wins the game.' Sudden death—it was the first time I'd ever heard the words *sudden death* on a football field. And I said, 'What the hell's going on? I'm tired, man; I just finished playing a football game.'"

Not yet, he hadn't. The Giants won the coin toss and elected to receive. They took possession on their 20 and once again came up a yard short on third down, forcing them to punt.

Members of the Giants and the Colts at a reunion of the men who played and coached in the Greatest Game Ever Played. Wellington Mara is kneeling at the right.

Baltimore also took over on its 20, but the Colts capitalized on their opportunity. L. G. DuPre ran for 11 yards to open the drive. Three plays later, Unitas threw an 8-yard pass to Ameche for a first down. A 21-yard pass to Berry put Baltimore on the Giants 43, and on the next play, Ameche ran up the middle for 20 more. The Giants were in serious trouble. A pass to Berry moved the ball to the 8. Ameche picked up a yard before Unitas's pass to tight end Jim Mutscheller put the ball on the 1. Generations of football fans have seen the black-and-white film of what happened next. Ameche took a handoff, ran over the right guard, and fell into the end zone for the winning points.

The immediate reaction for most Giants was to feel tremendous frustration at wasting an opportunity to win a championship. It was only in the days and weeks and even years that followed that the players came to understand they had participated in an epic sporting event. "I don't think any of us felt that that was the greatest game ever played," Summerall said. "And I think all of us had the idea that this was not the greatest game we ever played. Certainly we didn't play our best. And we didn't realize the magnitude of what it was—the overtime and the whole situation, until people started to write about it the next week."

The famed 1958 championship game was especially poignant for Wellington Mara. "That was the last game my father saw," Mara said. Tim Mara passed away on February 16, 1959. He did not see the Giants lose the championship game the following season in Baltimore, 31–16.

Like the players, Wellington Mara left Yankee Stadium not knowing the impact the game would have on the history of pro football. "You just looked at the game and no further," he said. But as he made his way around Manhattan in the days that followed, it became clear his team had been part of a very special event.

"The impact of the game around New York City was tremendous," Mara said. "Pete Rozelle often said if that game was played in Detroit or Green Bay or someplace, it wouldn't have had half the impact that it had here, because New York is the seat of all of the sponsors and national news services and everything. And he said that any place you went all that week all you heard about was the game, both before and after."

They still talk about it today.

The Bleak Years

John Mara doesn't remember where he was going, only that he had a terrible time getting there. He believes it was 1966, a year in which the Giants staggered to a 1–12–1 record under coach Allie Sherman. Mara, executive vice president and chief operating officer of the Giants, was a student at Our Lady of Sorrows grammar school in White Plains, New York. Never has a child attended a more appropriately named school.

The Giants of Mara's childhood were usually awful, a condition that continued when he went to Boston College. Because his father is Wellington Mara, who then ran the franchise, the team's problems resulted in many unpleasant moments for John. "I remember we were on a class trip and the bus went past Yankee Stadium [then the Giants' home]," Mara said. "The whole bus sang, 'Goodbye Allie.' As a kid, that has an effect on you."

It was also tough on a lot of other people, notably players, coaches, and fans. The Giants have been a hugely successful franchise since they were founded in 1925, with twenty-six playoff appearances and six championships. But the years from 1964 to 1980 were the darkest era in the organization's history. In those seventeen seasons, the team's combined record was 84–156–4. The Giants finished above .500 just twice, in 1970 and 1972. They did not make a postseason appearance.

During that period the Giants had five head coaches, four home stadiums, and a frequently changing cast of quarterbacks. They suffered some of the worst defeats in team history, including a game in which they surrendered an NFL-record 72 points and another, twelve years later, that ended with Joe Pisarcik's infamous fumble against the Philadelphia Eagles.

It's no wonder John Mara didn't feel like socializing the day after games. "I used to dread going to school on Monday mornings," he said. "After we had a bad Sunday, they [John Mara's schoolmates] would wait for him outside of school," Wellington Mara said. "We lived just a block and a half away, but I had to drive him to school on Monday mornings to make sure he'd go."

Those eighteen years were extremely difficult for Wellington Mara, whose life's work has been dedicated to improving the

Giants. During much of that period, Mara made the team's important football decisions. "At the time I was into it so much that I felt I knew exactly what had to be done to change things," Mara said. "I felt I was doing what was best and that was just a year away and so on—it just didn't work out that way. So, yeah, that was very, very difficult."

The Giants made a rapid descent from the penthouse to the basement. Sherman guided the team to championship games in 1961, 1962, and 1963—all losses. But the great defense at the heart of the team's success began to come apart. In 1962 Cliff Livingston traded. The following year it was Rosey Grier, and the year after that, Sam Huff and Dick Modzelewski. Many of the players that stayed quickly aged and lost their effectiveness. The result was a 2–10–2 record in 1964.

With a new quarterback in Earl Morrall and running back Tucker Fredrickson, the top pick in the 1965 draft, the Giants rallied to finish 7–7 in 1965. But Fredrickson missed the following season with a knee injury, and the Giants plummeted to a 1–12–1 record, the worst in franchise history. The chant of "Goodbye Allie" was popular not just on John Mara's school bus, but also in Yankee Stadium on football Sundays. "I thought they were lousy singers," Sherman said recently. "I must say, I didn't like hearing it. But I had only had one major concern: I didn't want it to affect my players."

The season's nadir occurred on November 27, when the Giants traveled to Washington to face the Redskins, a team they had defeated five weeks earlier for their only victory. The Redskins crushed them 72–41 in what is still the highest-scoring game in NFL history. Washington enjoyed a huge 28-point advantage when a time-out was called so Redskins kicker Charlie Gogolak could kick a 29-yard field goal with 3 seconds left.

Call it Sam Huff's revenge game. Prior to the 1964 season, Sherman had traded Huff to Washington for halfback Dick James and defensive end Andy Stynchula. It's a transaction that Huff has never gotten over. "As long as I live," Huff said, "I will never forgive Allie Sherman for trading me."

Before that game Huff told Washington quarterback Sonny Jurgensen, "This is get-even day." So with time winding down on the embarrassing defeat, Huff got his revenge. "I was on the sideline and I yelled for time out," Huff said. "[Coach] Otto Graham got credit for calling the time-out, but it was me. Charlie Gogolak goes in and kicks the field goal—72 points. I look across the field and I said, 'Justice is done.' I had my day. But it was like playing against your brother, which are the hardest fights you've ever had. I felt sorry for what I did, but not the result, because I had to get even."

Huff, by the way, didn't hold a grudge against Wellington Mara, whom he considers a dear friend. "He is really Mr. NFL," said Huff, who attends Giants-related functions in New York. "In the NFL, he has the highest respect an owner has ever had."

The Giants were 7–7 in both 1967 and 1968. Before the 1969 season Mara traded with Minnesota for Fran Tarkenton, one of the league's star quarterbacks. After an 0–5 preseason, Sherman was fired and replaced by Webster, who went 6–8 in his first season. In 1970 the Giants were 9–4 and needed to beat the Los Angeles Rams in Yankee Stadium in the season finale to clinch a playoff berth. But they lost 31–3 to finish 9–5.

Tarkenton played his final season for the Giants in 1971, when the team finished 4–10. He was then traded back to the

Vikings. Norm Snead took over in 1972, and the Giants finished 8–6. But that was as good as it got for a long time. They would not win more than six games in a season again until 1981.

"It was tough playing in those years," said linebacker Brian Kelley, who joined the team in 1973. "We had some good defenses. We had Harry Carson and Brad Van Pelt, John Mendenhall and Jack Gregory. But when people ask me who the quarterback was when I was playing, I lost count. We had Jerry Golsteyn, Jim DelGazio—people don't even remember him—Scott Brunner, Craig Morton, Joe Pisarcik. We almost had a different quarterback every year."

None of them is a threat to make the Hall of Fame. The Giants won two games in 1973, Webster's final season. Bill Arnsparger, the defensive coordinator on the Miami Dolphins' Super Bowl champions, took over as head coach. He won two games in his first season. The Giants improved to five victories in 1975, but when Arnsparger lost his first seven games in 1976, he was let go in favor of John McVay.

"We were a team that was floundering, and I dare say on all fronts," said defensive end George Martin, a rookie in 1975. "Bill Arnsparger was tabbed as a defensive genius, but that left a lot to be desired on the offensive side of the ball. He tried surrounding himself with an infusion of young talent. I think the first year eight of us that were drafted made the team. There wasn't much leadership back in those days. Or should I say there was the wrong type of leadership back in those days."

To add insult to losing, the Giants had to scramble to find a new home. They had grown tired of being second-class citizens in Yankee Stadium, where they couldn't play until the baseball

*Linebacker Brian Kelley,
who played for the Giants
from 1973 to 1983.*

season ended. "That meant six preseason games, plus the first two or three regular-season games on the road every year—we'd have eight or nine away games in a row," said Ed Croke, public relations director of the Giants from 1965 to 1992. "We had to pay rent, but we got no money from the concessions or parking."

Besides that, the famous ballpark wasn't a good football venue. So on August 27, 1971, the Giants signed a thirty-year lease with the New Jersey Sports and Exposition Authority to play in a new 75,000-seat stadium to be built just for them 5 miles from Manhattan. The news did not sit well with John Lindsay, mayor of New York. He had designs on a national office, and losing a popular NFL team would not look good on his résumé. Lindsay worried the Yankees might bolt next, so he decided to renovate Yankee Stadium. Of course that wasn't going to happen during the baseball season.

"We were left with no place to play," Wellington Mara said. "The mayor was a little put out with us and he put us out. [Team executive] Ray Walsh and I traveled all over the place. We visited [Princeton's] Palmer Stadium, Michie Stadium [at West Point], Randall's Island. But the people at Yale were very good to us." They also had 70,000 seats [in Yale Bowl], lots of parking, and plenty of hotel rooms nearby. The Giants were familiar with the stadium: Since 1969 their annual preseason game with the Jets had been played there.

The first time the teams had met, the Giants suffered a 37–14 defeat. In addition to the capacity crowd drawn by the game, New Haven hosted an American Legion convention that weekend. Not too far away, the Woodstock rock festival was being held, further choking the already clogged roads. "I think the worst memories I have of Yale Bowl was the game we played the Jets, and that was the weekend of big rock festival up in Woodstock," Mara said. "After getting really humiliated in the game, we had about a four-hour ride home."

After playing their first two home games in 1973 in Yankee Stadium, the Giants left for Yale Bowl, where they were 1–3. The following season, they lost all seven games in Connecticut. For those two years every game was a road game. The Giants would bus to New Haven on Saturday, stay in a hotel, then return after the game.

"We had a terrible team at the time," Mara said. "I think we struggled because we were practicing in Jersey City and playing our games in Connecticut, and we didn't really have a place we could call home. But it didn't affect the way Yale received us. That did influence my thinking when Leon Hess asked if the Jets could play in Giants Stadium. I know how much it meant to us to be able to go to Yale when we had no place to play."

In addition to being a far-away home, Yale Bowl presented the Giants with some unique challenges. The stadium had no locker rooms, so both the Giants and their opponents had to bus over to rooms in a field house about 300 yards away. "There was a halfway house on either side where the teams could go in at halftime and huddle around in what was nothing more than an oversized laundry room," Croke said.

Those players who unwisely chose to walk had to traverse a gauntlet of unhappy fans. (Remember, the Giants were 0–7 at home in 1974.) After one game running back Doug Kotar and Kelley decided to go by foot from the field to the locker room. A disgruntled fan started yelling at Kotar. Kelley turned and leveled the guy with a forearm. The commonsense-challenged fan stayed on the ground as Kelley stared him down and moved on.

Many NFL teams put up signs with inspirational messages in their locker rooms. At Yale that tradition took on a new twist for the Giants. They couldn't use the football team's locker room, so they dressed in a room used by some of school's women's teams. Arnsparger would try to get his team fired up with pep talks, a task made harder by signs on the walls with such rousing exhortations as BEAT BROWN, VANQUISH VASSAR, and ROUT RADCLIFFE.

In 1975 the Giants moved back to New York City—Abe Beame had replaced Lindsay as mayor—this time to Shea Stadium, then the home of the Mets and Jets. Even then Shea was a dank and depressing place. "When we were up at the Yale Bowl, it was like we were like nomadic players," Martin said. "We were barnstormers. It was terrible. Shea Stadium was an experience in and of itself. Shea was like a gladiator town. You had to walk through the dungeons and the cobwebs. I wasn't sure if we were supposed to return from the kill or what.

"We understood that there were new facilities on the horizon, that things were going to change, that there was a new commitment. But it was in the future, it was always in the future. So you were optimistic that if you could just survive and hang on until that point in time came, it would get better."

After playing their first four games of the 1976 season on the road, the Giants played their first game in beautiful new Giants Stadium on October 10. They lost to Dallas 24–14, but for the first time in their history, they had a home to call their own. The stadium did little to improve their fortunes on the field. Arnsparger was fired after a 27–0 loss to Pittsburgh. The following week, in McVay's first game, they failed to score again in a 10–0 loss to Philadelphia. The Giants finished the season 3–11.

The next year, a 3–3 start dissipated into a 5–9 finish. In 1978 the Giants had a 5–3 record midway through the season. But they lost seven of their last eight games, including one of the most inexplicable and embarrassing defeats in franchise history.

On November 19 the Giants hosted their archrivals, the Philadelphia Eagles. The Giants led 17–12 when Odis McKinney's interception gave them the ball at their own 21 with just 1:23 remaining. All they had to do was fall on the ball three times and the upset victory would be theirs. Pisarcik took a knee on first down, losing 3 yards. Larry Csonka then gained 11 yards, setting up a third and 2 at the 29 with 31 seconds remaining. Another kneel-down by Pisarcik and the game would safely be finished. McVay was so sure that's what would happen, he took off his headset. He had no idea what was about to unfold.

To the shock of all the offensive players on the field, Bob Gibson sent in a play that called for another handoff to Csonka. The players in the huddle—most notably center Jim Clack—told Pisarcik to defy the order and take a knee. But Pisarcik, who had frequently butted heads with Gibson, feared he'd be benched if he didn't do as he was told.

Once the play was called and the players went to the line of scrimmage, the Eagles defensive linemen asked Clack what was coming. They didn't want to get hurt. If Clack had said they were taking a knee, Philly's front would have relaxed and gone home. "Do you believe we're going to run a play?" Clack said. They didn't, but it was coming anyway. Pisarcik spun around and tried to hand off to Csonka. The ball hit Csonka's knee and bounced

Nine-time Pro Bowl linebacker Harry Carson closes in on a ballcarrier.

Proper Credit?

Not long after the Giants beat the Denver Broncos in Super Bowl XXI to cap the 1986 season, public relations man Ed Croke ran into former quarterback Joe Pisarcik, who lost the infamous last-minute fumble against Philadelphia in 1978.

Pisarcik said he deserved to be thanked for his role in helping the Giants get to the Super Bowl. "He said, 'If I didn't fumble, McVay wouldn't have been fired, George Young wouldn't have been hired, and neither would Parcells,'" Croke said.

Pisarcik told him, "I'm the guy responsible for all that happening."

in the air. Philadelphia cornerback Herm Edwards (now head coach of the Jets) caught it in stride and went into the end zone for an unbelievable winning touchdown.

"Just when you think you can't get any lower, something like that happens to you," said Brad Benson, who was playing tackle. "It was stunning. It was not Pisarcik's fault. They told him specifically to hand that ball off."

"I remember distinctly high-fiving my teammates on the sideline, because we thought the game was won," Martin said. "There was a sense of elation. It was a victory, and they were few and far between. And all of a sudden, this happens, and 76,000 people and fifty-five players are absolutely mortified, petrified, stunned in disbelief. And I've heard that term so often since then. But we probably coined that phrase 'stunned in disbelief' because that's exactly what we were. We couldn't speak. And that's what I think formed the empathy I will always have with the Boston baseball team. They always talked about Jimmy Hoffa and his curse, and we believed it. We absolutely believed it. We were cursed. I mean, that was evidence right there. We couldn't win to save our lives."

Harry Carson kept staring at the field, in absolute disbelief at what he had just witnessed. "I couldn't move," he said. "When the game was over, I stayed on the bench for about fifteen, twenty minutes in shock," he said. "I couldn't believe it. I think the fumble was probably a low point for every Giants fan. Things happen for a reason, but you don't want to be a part of something like that when it is happening."

Before the shock lessened, the dominoes started falling. Gibson was fired the next day. (Benson said it was immediately after the game. "I saw him carrying his stuff out and I hadn't hit the shower yet," he said.) McVay was let go at the end of the season. Fewer than three months after "The Fumble," George Young was hired as general manager, the move that started the franchise's reversal of fortunes. Young hired Ray Perkins as head coach and, in 1981, the Giants made the playoffs for the first time in eighteen years. Five years later, they were Super Bowl champions under Bill Parcells.

The Crunch Bunch

More than 1,200 players have been part of the Giants' family in the more than eighty-year history of the franchise. Some, such as Phil Simms and George Martin, remained for more than a decade and established roots to last a lifetime. Many more stayed only long enough to enjoy the NFL equivalent of a cup of coffee.

Across those many years hundreds of friendships were formed. Some lasted only as long as the players wore the same uniform, then evaporated forever. Others took on a heartwarming permanence. The five offensive linemen from the 1986 Super Bowl champions—collectively known as "The Suburbanites"—are almost as close today as when they shared a huddle twenty years ago.

But no group of one-time Giants has retained a bond as strong as that formed by four linebackers who played together in the late 1970s and early 1980s: Harry Carson, Brad Van Pelt, Brian Kelley, and Lawrence Taylor. They were called the "Crunch Bunch," a fierce and punishing collection of players who at first shined during the Giants' dark period and, then in 1981 helped lift the team to its first playoff berth in eighteen years. The group cemented its tough-as-titanium reputation by posing for a poster at a construction site, with all four players wearing hardhats. The poster was a must-have item for Giants fans.

All these years later, the four men remain as close as brothers. They speak to each other regularly on the phone. There are frequent golf outings, numerous autograph shows, and road trips. They have vacationed in Bermuda together. Every year the foursome travels to Hawaii at Pro Bowl time to play some golf, enjoy some beach time, and retell the old stories.

In October 2004 at Carson's urging, the Crunch Bunch came together for a far different activity. The four men spent a day in Puebla, a city in central Mexico, where they were among 3,000 or so volunteers helping to build houses for Habitat for Humanity, the international nonprofit housing ministry made famous by former president Jimmy Carter. Three months later, they headlined an event in Manhattan dubbed the "Heavy Hitters," which honored the finest linebackers in Giants' history: the Crunch Bunch, plus Sam Huff and Carl Banks.

"It is sort of like a brotherhood," Carson said. "We, as a group, were considered during our time probably the best group of linebackers in the league. We played for one another and had a tremendous sense of pride in our unit as a group. We have done a lot of stuff on the field, but also we did a lot of stuff off the field. In essence we bonded tremendously, and I would venture to say at one point we were probably the best linebacker corps in the NFL. That is something that doesn't fade overnight or through the years. You recognize that we were really a good group of players who played well together.

"Now, when we go somewhere together, I think what happens is we assume the roles that we had when we played. We are four guys who genuinely like one another. We played together. We went through a lot of good stuff together; we went through some bad stuff together. We bonded. But I think it is good that we can keep this relationship going."

"We're all different," Taylor said. "I think we all have different personalities. But we all enjoy the same thing. We all enjoy playing the game of football. We enjoy the insaneness of football and what comes with the game. You look at our personalities and we're all different, but we just bond. Maybe opposites attract."

Whenever the Crunch Bunch comes together there are plenty of laughs, good-natured putdowns, storytelling, and reminiscing. Said Kelley: "Don't come there with thin skin. It's still the same as locker room talk. It's amazing. We go to the Pro Bowl together, and we play golf every day with each other, and we just enjoy each other's company. I would be surprised if there are four other linebackers that have that kind of relationship. We played a lot of years together. We were very fortunate to be able to do something like that and that bonded us."

A particularly favorite story is the time Leon Perry pulverized Taylor during practice in the linebacker's rookie season. It was one of the few times anyone ever got the best of Taylor on the football field. "Leon Perry was a short, studly fullback," Kelley said. "L. T. came on a blitz and I tell you, Leon Perry hit him and knocked his wristbands off and turned his helmet completely around. He was looking out of the ear hole of his helmet, and he was wobbling. It was a shot and it was so loud. That always comes up when L. T. starts to get a little bigheaded."

The story has been told a hundred times, from restaurants in New Jersey to golf courses in Honolulu. Like fraternity brothers catching up at a reunion, the Crunch Bunch never tires of retelling tall tales.

"I've known Brad for thirty-two years, Harry for twenty-nine, and L. T. for twenty-four years," Kelley said. "How do you explain those relationships? We have the same relationship off the field we had on the field. We had the trust of each other. When I was on the field, I knew Brad wasn't going to let the tight end come off and hit me. When you have trust like that on the field—it's the same with L. T. and Harry—I think it just evolves off the field. We trust each other that we're not going to take advantage of each other, that we're not going to take advantage of L. T.'s fame. He knows that he has three friends that he can call when he wants to speak to someone."

"I love it—for those few moments, I get to relive part of the good times in my life," Van Pelt said. "I feel as comfortable with

*Linebacker Brad Van Pelt,
who played in five Pro Bowls
as a Giant.*

them as I do with my brothers. Obviously, your brothers are your brothers. But these three are probably the closest thing to them. Brian and I played eleven years together. I played nine with Harry. Lawrence being the guy, it didn't take long for him to fit right in and become one of the guys. I can't really explain why but they're the only three [former teammates] I stay close with."

The group began forming in 1973, when the Giants selected Van Pelt in the first round of the NFL draft out of Michigan State and Kelley in the fourteenth round from Cal Lutheran. Three years later, Carson joined the team as a fourth-round pick. In the five seasons from 1976 to 1980, Van Pelt made five Pro Bowls and Carson two, while the linebackers were the best unit on teams that won a total of just twenty-four games.

"I had to allow those guys to help me to a certain degree because I had never played linebacker until I came to the Giants," said Carson, a defensive lineman at South Carolina State. "Brian got shifted over to outside linebacker and I played the middle. I had to rely on his expertise and his experience to help me until I was able to get my bearings straight. I remember watching Brad even before I came to the Giants. I knew about Brad when he was at Michigan State, playing a rover back, wearing number 10. I thought it was really special to have the opportunity to play with him. With Brian I was really impressed with his intellect and his knowledge of the game. I think the odd man out was Pat Hughes, who was a solid linebacker, but the Giants felt they needed more help stopping the run inside, so that's where I played. Brian was too valuable to be put on the bench so he got shifted to the outside. We played well together for a few years, and then Lawrence came in, and the rest is history."

All of it good. In 1981 the Giants used the second pick in the draft to secure Taylor, who would become the dominant defensive player of his era during a thirteen-year career that earned him a bust in the Pro Football Hall of Fame.

Taylor initially received a chilly reception from the three incumbent linebackers. The Giants had finished 4–12 in 1980, when Carson, Van Pelt, and Kelley made up what was the finest unit on the team. With so many other glaring needs, the last thing the trio thought the team needed was another linebacker. Taylor, an All-America linebacker at the University of North Carolina, got wind of the grumbling prior to the draft and publicly suggested it might not be in everybody's best interest for the Giants to draft him. But there was no chance the Giants would select another player if Taylor was available. George Young, the general manager, and the personnel department had Taylor rated as the best player in the country. Taylor was coming to New Jersey, whether Carson and his mates liked it or not.

"We felt we didn't need another linebacker," Carson said. "[Running back] George Rogers was going to be the Giants' first pick. As it turned out, New Orleans had that first pick, and they drafted Rogers. Lawrence got wind of the fact that we were sort of bitching and complaining about the Giants drafting him. He sort of sent us a message through the media . . . if there was going to be a problem, just don't draft him. And so when they drafted him, they brought him in, we met him, he was cool. I think at the time we said it had nothing to do with him personally. We just thought that we needed to have our needs filled, and linebacker wasn't necessarily the weakness that needed to be addressed. But he was the best athlete available, and the Giants went after him."

The Giants switched to a 3–4 defense so Taylor could start with Carson, Van Pelt, and Kelley. And it took less than five minutes on the practice field for Taylor to demonstrate to everyone that drafting him was one of the wisest personnel decisions in franchise history. "I'll never forget it," Van Pelt said. "I was pissed off because I was coming off my fifth Pro Bowl in a row and they signed him to a million-dollar bonus and the guy's making nearly two times what I'm making. The guy hadn't even put a helmet on and he was making that much more money than me. Then I watched him one day in practice and said, 'Okay, he's worth it.' He's just a rare individual. The ability he had—I still think back to how amazing it was to watch him on film. He was actually stepping right with the snap of the ball. Everybody else was still [at] a standstill, he was moving toward the ball—that's amazing."

"It is well documented that before Lawrence got there we felt pretty good within ourselves that we were a good group of line-backers," Carson said. "Then when Lawrence got there, we all saw his talent, and he just made us even better than what we thought we could be."

In his first intrasquad scrimmage, L. T., as he quickly became known, had 4 sacks and a fumble recovery. He dominated his preseason debut with 10 solo tackles, 2 sacks, and a fumble recovery. During the course of his rookie season, Taylor established himself as the NFL's most dominant defensive player. When the season ended, he had 133 tackles and 9.5 sacks, and the Giants had ended eighteen years of futility with a playoff berth. With that kind of impact, Taylor easily found himself a place at the table with the close-knit group of linebackers.

"It was great to play together," Carson said. "I played with Brad and Brian for five seasons before Lawrence got there. So I knew how to work off of them. Then when Lawrence came, I had to learn to play off of Lawrence. And Lawrence had to learn to play off me. During the course of a play or in a game, certain things happen and you react as a football player. With Lawrence, he would sometimes move his area of responsibility and I would fill for him. Or, if I did something, he would fill for me. And we knew each other's responsibility and we played off one another. I think that is one of the good things. Because there were plays where we would screw up, but we would still recover in time that nobody would notice that there was a problem. Like I said, we were able to play off of one another. And Brad and Brian were the same way."

The linebackers were even close numerically—well, at least three of them were. Carson wore uniform number 53, Kelley was 55, and Taylor was 56, which the Giants retired in 1994. Van Pelt, however, wore number 10 and never had any desire to complete the straight by requesting 54.

"I played three sports in high school, and I wore 10 in all three," Van Pelt said. "Everything in my athletic career was going very well. I'm very superstitious so I was hoping 10 would be available when I was drafted by the Giants. They were supposed to give me a number in the 50s or 90s. But I was also a backup kicker in college, and I was the Giants' backup kicker my rookie year. They said, 'The league might give us a problem, but we'll give you number 10 as a kicker who happens to play linebacker.'

I got to wear that number. I was a quarterback in high school, and I went to Michigan State as a quarterback, so I wore 10. It helped my career. I got to be a better linebacker and I started getting noticed a little more—that number, they couldn't forget it. It's been a lucky number for me. I was very fortunate the Giants allowed me to have it."

It didn't bring him good luck early in his career. From 1973, the year Kelley and he joined the team, through 1979, the Giants' record was 29–72–1. Carson's arrival in 1976 did nothing to change the team's fortunes. But Taylor's did. The year he began terrorizing opposing quarterbacks, the Giants won five more games than they had the previous season, improving to 9–7 in 1981 and earning a wild-card playoff berth. They beat the defending NFC-champion Eagles in Philadelphia for their first postseason victory since 1958 before falling the following week to San Francisco.

"For Brad and me, it was our ninth season, and it was just tremendous," Kelley said of the unexpected success. "That's what we'd been playing for the whole time. To finally accomplish that—it was great to finally get to the playoffs. It was even greater when we went down to Philadelphia and beat the crap out of the Eagles down there in Philly. We lost to the Niners, who eventually won the Super Bowl, but it was a great feeling to finally accomplish something. We were headed in the right direction."

Not for long. The Giants were 4–5 in the strike-gutted 1982 season, and they sustained an emotional hit late in the season when coach Ray Perkins announced he was leaving for the University of Alabama. After a 3–12–1 disaster in 1983, new coach

Bill Parcells got rid of several veteran players, including Van Pelt and Kelley. Van Pelt played briefly for the Raiders and Browns, while Kelley left the game.

"The nice thing about leaving New York and going to the Raiders and eventually to Cleveland, I found out just how special the Giants' organization is," Van Pelt said. "There isn't a better organization in all of professional sports than the New York Giants."

After the departure of the two originals, Carson and Taylor soldiered on with new linebacker mates, including Carl Banks, Pepper Johnson, and Gary Reasons. In 1986 the Giants had the NFL's best team and won the Super Bowl for the first time. For Carson winning a title in his eleventh season was an accomplishment that brought him pure joy. But amid the celebration, he remembered Kelley and Van Pelt, his two friends who didn't stay long enough to earn a ring.

"I enjoyed the spoils for them," Carson said. "When we went to the Super Bowl and we won, I reflected on all of the guys who didn't make it to that point. Brad and Brian were two of those guys who laid the groundwork for what happened later in the '80s. It's a shame they couldn't have been a part of it, because they played their hearts out while they were with the Giants. They helped me become the player that I became and also pushed Lawrence to become the player that he did."

Carson retired following the 1988 season, a year after being selected to the last of his nine Pro Bowls. Taylor won another Super Bowl ring in 1990, the year he went to his tenth and final Pro Bowl. He returned from a torn Achilles tendon in 1992 to play well and lead the Giants to a playoff berth in 1993, then announced his retirement immediately after a playoff loss in San Francisco.

"Lawrence and I were there, and we never forgot about Brad and Brian, but in a way we sort of added Carl and Gary to the mix as extensions to what we had," Carson said. "I think the bottom line is that the Giants had been known at the time for defense — a strong defense—and that goes back to the '50s with [Sam] Huff and [Andy] Robustelli and all of those guys. As linebackers we felt that we had a legacy to uphold. Brad did a great job and he made five Pro Bowls. Brian never made a Pro Bowl, but Brian really was, at the time, the quarterback. He was sort of the brains of the outfit. Lawrence did his thing. I was sort of that hard-hat sort of guy who just tried to be consistent. We all had our ways of getting things done."

In their postfootball lives, the members of the Crunch Bunch separated but remained friendly. They have supported each other in tough times; all of them, for example, endured a divorce. In recent years they have participated in more and more events, such as autograph signings and golf tournaments, as a group. Carson remains the leader of the group, and he is at the forefront of organizing trips and ensuring the four stay together. "They know they can count on me, and I know that I can count on them," Carson said. "We just have a special bond, and it is kind of difficult to describe it. We all like one another. We have never been jealous of anyone's success. I think that we all understand each other's strengths, but also I think we understand each other's weaknesses."

An indication of Carson's influence is that he convinced Van Pelt, Kelley, and Taylor to travel to Puebla, Mexico, to participate in the Habitat for Humanity build. Since it was founded in 1976, Habitat has built more than 150,000 houses around the world, providing more than 750,000 people in more than 3,000 communities with safe, decent, affordable shelter. The homes are built with volunteer labor and donations of money and materials.

Carson got involved as a spokesperson for Medeco, the company that provides the locks for Habitat for Humanity homes. Medeco's CEO, Bob Cook, invited Carson to a build in the South Bronx, near Yankee Stadium. Carson enlisted some members of the Giants' organization and wound up visiting the site several times. Cook then asked Carson if he would participate in a build in Mexico in a Jimmy Carter work project. Carson agreed in a New York minute and vowed to involve the rest of the Crunch Bunch.

"I thought it would be a good opportunity for us to get together and give back, and get our name out there, and bring some exposure to Habitat and also Medeco," Carson said. "First I ran it past Bob. He said that if I could swing it, then Medeco would pay the expenses. So I ran it past Brian, and Brian said yes. And I ran it past Brad; Brad said yes. And I called Lawrence, because I knew Lawrence was going to be the hard sell. I said, 'Lawrence, I need you for a day. You are not going to be paid for it, and you are not going to gripe and complain.' And I told him what it was, and I told him that Brad, Brian, and I were in, and he said, 'Okay.'"

Getting Taylor to utter that one word is usually the tallest hurdle to his involvement in any Crunch Bunch endeavor. "The biggest problem is getting him there," Kelley said. "The three of us always have the biggest headache—is he going to show or not?

Hall of Famer Lawrence
Taylor enjoys a relaxing
moment at training camp.

Once you get him to any event, he really gets into it and he goes all out, like he did on the football field. That's what he does, and that's exactly what happened."

The members of the Crunch Bunch arrived at the house with varying degrees of experience. Van Pelt had worked on construction throughout college and still does a fair amount of work on his family's homes in northern Michigan. "The guys were kidding me, because I came with my tool belt," he said. Carson is a skilled handyman who has an account at Home Depot. Kelley can do some work, but not on the level of Van Pelt and Carson. Those three, however, all came dressed for the job.

And then there was Taylor. Carson had told him to bring work clothes. So there was Taylor, wearing black golf slacks, a white shirt, and a black vest. He looked like he was ready to play thirty-six holes, not pour cement. "It was a pretty simple explanation that he gave," Kelley said. "He told us, 'They said to wear my work clothes. This is what I wear every day for work. So I wore my golf clothes.' It's pretty simple and he was right. That's Lawrence. But I'll tell you what, he worked his butt off. I give him credit."

"Of the four of us, I thought Lawrence would have a more difficult time dealing with the situation," Carson said. "But the reality was that Lawrence gravitated to it better. He really got into it and really was gung ho about doing it. He really got into a flow. It is funny. When you see him in the pictures, we told him to wear work clothes and he brought golf attire. He said, 'That is what I work in.' But he had no bones about working, pouring cement, working in mastic, and being up on a scaffold, wearing those black golf pants and white shirt. Once he got into it, he didn't want to break for lunch. We had to force him to break for lunch. And at the end of the day, he didn't want to leave."

The four former Giants were assigned to a house in which a woman named Sonia and her three children would live. Carson and Company poured cement, laid bricks, sanded walls, and performed numerous other tasks. Sonia was there helping. When they departed that night, the men who had once created mayhem on a football field had made significant progress in helping a woman and her children occupy their dream house.

"The Crunch Bunch did all right," Van Pelt said. "When we joined the project, they were a little behind, and by the end of the day, we were ahead. They actually took us off and sent us to other places to help them in different places where they were behind."

After coming together in New York, Hawaii, or Mexico, the foursome splits up until their next meeting. Van Pelt now lives in his native Michigan, while Taylor has settled in Florida. Carson and Kelley, like Phil Simms, George Martin, and many other players, came to New Jersey to join the Giants and have never left. In the case of Kelley, a native Californian, his decision to remain in the Garden State was aided by a mandate Perkins gave him a quarter-century ago.

"The story of how I ended up on the East Coast is sort of funny," Kelley said. "I was still living on the West Coast and commuting back and forth for the season. I was also playing rugby in the off-season . . . I played for the Santa Monica Rugby Club. We played for the national championship in Monterey, California. We won the national championship and I scored the winning try—a try is like a touchdown. It so happened that I was on the front page of the sports section in Monterey and in San Francisco.

"The next day, I got a call from Ray Perkins. He said, 'Boy, what are you doing playing rugby?' I said, 'No one told me I couldn't play rugby.' And he said, 'Well, I'm telling you, you aren't playing rugby anymore. You might as well pack your bags, because you're moving to the East Coast.' That was pretty much it, and I did move. I was an East Coaster after that. I've been here since 1980. I love it here."

When you're a member of the Crunch Bunch, what's not to love?

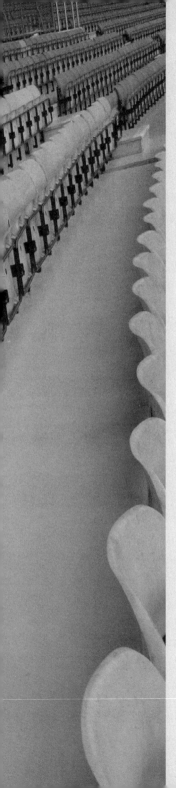

The Great Eighties

No one with an interest in the Giants could have predicted in the months prior to the 1984 season that the franchise was about to embark on one of the most successful eras in team history. The 1983 season had been a disaster; the Giants finished 3–12–1 under first-year head coach Bill Parcells. George Young considered replacing Parcells with Howard Schnellenberger, but he decided to stick with the coach who had distinguished himself as defensive coordinator.

Given new life, Parcells became a better coach. When he spoke to his team for the first time in '84, he delivered a powerful message that he and the team were going to change. "He put his heart on his sleeve," said linebacker Carl Banks. "He said, 'Guys, we have some bad players and bad characters on this team, and I'm going to get rid of some guys. You know who you are. You're hurting my team.' He said, 'I need guys who want to win, because if I don't win this year, I'm going to be fired.' He took a big risk. He got rid of a lot of talented players. He was demanding. That was sort of the first brick in the winning foundation when he stood in front of the team."

Guard Bill Ard said, "He was becoming Bill Parcells. He started swinging the hammer." And he started reshaping his roster. Van Pelt and Kelley were replaced by younger and faster players Byron Hunt, Gary Reasons, and Banks, then a rookie. Phil Simms was installed as the starting quarterback and threw for a team-record 4,044 yards. Joe Morris began to regularly carry the ball. Lawrence Taylor had 11.5 sacks.

"It took the threat of losing my job to get me to say, 'I'm doing this my way,'" Parcells said. "That included changing a lot of players in '84. I told them there are going to be changes, and hopefully the results are going to be different. Eighty-four was one of the hardest training camps anyone's ever been through. But I had a good nucleus of competitive guys there. There were some talented players."

That season the Giants went 9–7 and earned an NFC wild-card berth, the first step in a great seven-year run. From 1984 to 1990, the Giants' regular-season record was 74–37. They won three NFC East titles, made five trips to the playoffs, and won two

Bill Parcells by the Numbers

Here's the year-by-year Giants record under head coach Bill Parcells:

Year	Record	Postseason
1983	3–12–1	–
1984	9–7–0 (NFC wild card)	1–1
1985	10–6–0 (NFC wild card)	1–1
1986	14–2–0 (Division champion)	3–0 (won Super Bowl XXI)
1987	6–9–0	–
		–
1988	10–6–0	–
		–
1989	12–4–0 (Division champion)	0–1
1990	13–3–0 (Division champion)	3–0 (won Super Bowl XXV)
TOTALS	77–49–1	8–3

Super Bowls. Their only losing season was in 1987, when they were 6–9 and dropped three games in which they used replacement players during a strike.

Those teams were put together by the late George Young, general manager of the Giants. Young drafted Phil Simms and

Phil Simms, the greatest quarterback in Giants history.

Lawrence Taylor in the first round and Joe Morris in the second. He hired first Ray Perkins and then Parcells as coach. For almost two decades Young made the decisions that shaped the Giants. After leaving the Giants he was the NFL's vice president of football operations until his death on December 8, 2001.

"George was more than a general manager," Harry Carson said. "He was a teacher. He didn't care just about the game, the league, and the team, he also cared about the players. George wanted us to look at the game as a springboard and a stepping-stone to other things, to our lives after football. He wanted to get players to look at the big picture. I strongly admired and respected the man. George had a gruff exterior. But deep down inside he had a heart of gold and was a teddy bear."

The Giants enjoyed a taste of postseason success in 1984, defeating the Rams in Los Angeles in an NFC wild-card playoff game. The following week they played well before losing to the eventual Super Bowl champion 49ers in San Francisco, 21–10. "Eighty-four was the year we turned things around," Parcells said. "We had a chance to beat the Niners there that day. It wasn't a great chance, but we had a chance. I knew we were going to be pretty good after that."

That game ratcheted up the intensity in what became the NFL's best interdivisional rivalry. In the ten seasons from 1981 to 1990, the Giants and 49ers met twelve times, including five post-season meetings. The Giants were 1–6 in the regular season, but 3–2 in the playoffs, with victories in the last three games, including a 49–3 rout in 1986 and a 15–13 victory in the epic 1990 NFC Championship Game. But in 1984 the Giants were crushed at home by San Francisco in a Monday night game, then thought the Niners were arrogant during the playoff contest. They never forgot as the teams met in a series of tense, highly competitive games.

"The Niners were really afraid of us a little bit as we went on through the years," Parcells said. "They really didn't like us that much. I know. Their players would tell me. I know [Joe] Montana well and Ronnie Lott—I know those kids. They really didn't want to play us that much."

"We left that game very angry," Banks said, speaking of the 1984 playoff game. "We weren't thinking, 'Wow, the better team won.' I don't know if we felt we were better, but we thought we could beat them. We knew the next time we played them we would beat them."

They were correct. The following year, the Giants hosted the 49ers in the wild-card round and won easily, 17–3. As a reward the Giants traveled to Chicago, who were 15–1 and featured one of history's best defenses that season. On a frigid, windy day in Soldier Field, the Giants fell, 21–0. "That was absolutely the coldest game I ever played in," Banks said. "It was brutal. It was numbing. I grew up in Michigan, but I've never been that cold in my life."

"I remember warming up and saying, 'I'm not wearing gloves,'" Simms said. "I thought I could throw without them. I went out and I'm not exaggerating, within one minute I had another shirt on and I put those gloves right on. It was the first time I ever tried them. It was great. I threw the hell out of it. But there was no choice. It was too cold."

The team's frustration was personified by Sean Landeta, who went to punt the ball and whiffed. Chicago's Shaun Gayle picked it up and returned it 5 yards for the game's first touchdown. After seeing the Bears crush the Rams and New England Patriots on their way to the championship, the Giants were convinced they were the NFL's second-best team in 1985. "We just couldn't get past Chicago," Parcells said.

When the 1986 season opened, the Giants thought they had a special group, though they knew competition in the NFC would be fierce. Simms, the best quarterback in team history, and Lawrence Taylor, the best outside linebacker to ever play, were in their prime. Joe Morris had hit his stride as a top-flight running back. The lineup included Pro Bowlers such as Banks, Harry Carson, and Mark Bavaro. The team also had many valuable complementary players, most notably the offensive linemen. Collectively, the group was known as the "Suburbanites." Brad Benson, Bill Ard, Bart Oates, Chris Godfrey, and Karl Nelson were affable and friendly, the kind of guys you would enjoy having as neighbors in an average bedroom community.

The Giants began the '86 season with a Monday night loss in Dallas. They won their next five games before losing a mistake-filled affair in Seattle. In the postgame locker room, Taylor went on a rampage, throwing his equipment around the room and cursing at high volume. "I'm telling you," Taylor said, "we're not losing another game."

Remarkably, they didn't. Morris rushed for 181 yards two weeks in a row as the Giants beat division rivals Washington and Dallas. After a 17–14 win in Philadelphia, they headed for Minnesota on November 16. Raul Allegre kicked five field goals in a 22–20 victory. But the game is best remembered for the play that set up Allegre's game-winning 33-yarder with 12 seconds left. A minute earlier, the Giants needed a first down to keep the drive alive, a seemingly impossible task considering they faced a fourth

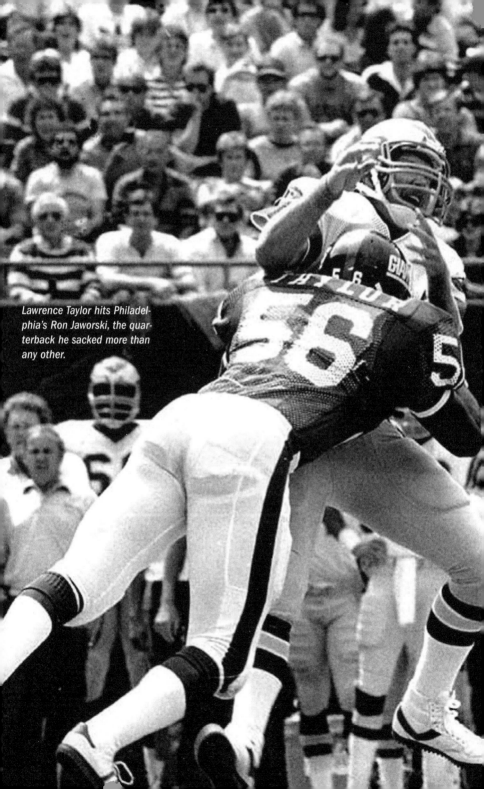

Lawrence Taylor hits Philadelphia's Ron Jaworski, the quarterback he sacked more than any other.

and 17 from their own 48 yard line. But after a time out, Simms hit Bobby Johnson on the right sideline for a 22-yard gain that immediately went down in Giants' lore as one of the greatest plays in franchise history.

"I can remember the play exactly. It was probably one of the first plays we put in every training camp. It actually gave me three options down the field. Back then, you had so many plays that were designed to go deep. When you got in those situations, it wasn't that big of a deal. I remember the discussion between Bill, [receivers coach] Pat Hodgson, and [offensive coordinator] Ron Erhardt. They told me the play, and I said, 'Yeah, that gives us the best chance.' I was going to look for Phil McConkey on the seam. It was covered. I was going to look for Lionel Manuel coming deep over the middle. I can remember breaking the huddle and saying to Bobby Johnson, 'If I get in trouble, make sure you stay right on the sideline, and I'll try to get it to you if I have to.' Because I figured they were going to play a defense that was going to give me some seams in it—I was going to have to find those seams. They took away the first two. It's a good thing I said that, and I realized at the last second that I had Bobby on the sideline. I saw it and hit him.

"I never realized how close it was. [Cornerback] Issiac Holt missed the ball by about half an inch. As I threw the ball, I got hit and went to the ground, but I knew it was going to be complete. When it left, right away I knew it was perfect."

The locker room celebration was unusually raucous. At 9–2 the players began to think a championship was in their future. Parcells said that game was when he began thinking that team and that season could be very special. "We still had six games to go, but

I figured we were going to be hard to beat," he said. "I told the team, 'The season starts now.' I said, 'We should win here, let's go.' And they did. They kept winning."

"That was the crowning moment when doubt was eradicated," said defensive end George Martin, who was then a twelve-year veteran. "We had a sense of purpose, and they used the term a sense of destiny. We felt it; we believed in it. And that's when champions were born, on that date. We were crowned in the Super Bowl, but we came of age that day."

Martin, one of the most respected players on the team, was the hero the following week in a 19–16 victory over Denver. Allegre's field goal in the final minutes, his fourth of the game, won it.

The Broncos led 6–3 and were driving for another score late in the first half when Martin intercepted a John Elway pass and took off. Escorted by what seemed like the ten other defensive players, Martin shook off Elway's attempted tackle, then rumbled for what felt like five minutes on his way to a 78-yard touchdown. "That's the greatest play I've ever been around," Parcells said. "That was a thirty-three-year-old guy doing that, making a one-handed interception. He dodges, fakes an option, runs up the sideline—oh, what a play."

"I always fancied myself more as a receiver because I was a tight end in college," said Martin, who set an NFL record with 6 touchdowns as a defensive lineman. "There were a lot of games where I'd warm up Phil. I wanted to touch the football once in awhile. I had an affinity for the football. That play incorporated my athleticism and, obviously, my ability to catch the ball. But it was really a team effort. Because there was no way I could have gotten to the end zone without the blocks I received. It was just an improbable play."

The following week, the Giants played on Monday night in San Francisco and trailed at halftime 17–0. No problem. They scored 21 unanswered points in the third period to win, 21–17. "The second touchdown we scored, I threw a long one down the right sideline to Stacy Robinson for a touchdown," Simms said. "As we do it, somebody jumps on my back and is celebrating. That was okay, I was into that. I turned around and it was [guard] Billy Ard. I was like, 'Wow, we are into this. Billy is fired up; this is great.' We're getting ready to get on the plane and I said, 'Billy, I've never seen you that fired up about a game.' He said, 'Aw hell, Phil, I only jumped on you because I knew the cameras would be on you and I wanted to be on TV.'"

It was about this time that the Giants devised an unusual celebration for each victory. As time wound down, Carson would pick up a large orange bucket of Gatorade and empty its contents over Parcells's head. Nose tackle Jim Burt was actually the first to do it, following a week in which he had taken all kinds of verbal abuse from Parcells. Carson kept it going and even dumped a Gatorade bucket full of popcorn on the head of Ronald Reagan when the Giants visited the White House.

"The reason why I had to keep doing it was because everybody knew that Bill was superstitious," Carson said. "If you do something and it works, you have to keep doing it. We were winning, so I kept giving him this shower."

He couldn't skip a week, because the Giants kept winning. On December 14 the Giants won a battle of 11–2 teams when they intercepted 6 passes and defeated the Redskins 24–14, clinching the NFC East. They finished the regular season with resounding victories over St. Louis (27–7) and Green Bay (55–24).

"With that team I was always confident on defense," Parcells said. "I knew we were going to be hard to score on. And I knew if we ever got a 10-point lead, it was over. Because that's when the dogs would get loose." The top dog was Taylor, who had a career-high 20.5 sacks and was a unanimous selection as the NFL's most valuable player.

"The thing that stands out in my mind was the commitment of everybody on that team," Carson said. "Guys were very unselfish, checking their egos at the door and playing for one another. I had never really been part of a team that had been so unselfish. I think the greatness of that team was that we all played together. Whatever differences we had, it really didn't matter. We were on a mission, and we all hurt from that loss to the Bears. By the end of the season, everything was clicking. The mental mistakes were gone. We beat people into submission physically. I would have hated to play against that team, because everybody knew what their role was, and we had that sense of confidence."

That was apparent when the Giants welcomed their old friends, the 49ers, to Giants Stadium for a divisional playoff game. If San Francisco carried any lingering arrogance, it was crushed in a 49–3 romp. In the NFC Championship Game against Washington, the Giants won the coin toss and elected to kick off to take advantage of the twenty-five-mile-per-hour winds. The Redskins went down to a 17–0 defeat as the fans in Giants Stadium went wild.

The victory put the Giants in Super Bowl XXI against the Broncos, whom they had narrowly defeated two months earlier. After falling behind 10–9 at halftime, the Giants put 30 points on the board in the second half and rolled to a 39–20 triumph for their first title in thirty years. "That was as well as one of my teams has ever played in a sustained stretch," Parcells said of the 12–0 run following the loss in Seattle.

Simms had the best game any quarterback has ever played in the Super Bowl, completing 22 of 25 passes (88 percent) for 268 yards and 3 touchdowns. In the second half Simms, who won the MVP award in a landslide, hit all 10 of his passes. "He was magnificent," Parcells said. "They dropped two passes on him, or he would have hit all but one."

"I remember warming up before the game and it was really hot," Simms said. "That was probably the first time we ever orchestrated some opening plays. I didn't ever have any idea what the first play of the game was going to be. Whatever hit Ron, that's what he went with. But that game we scripted quite a few plays that we wanted to run on the first drive. And a lot of them went the way we wanted. I don't remember throwing a ball I thought should be incomplete. I didn't realize until somebody told me in the locker room that I didn't throw an incompletion in the second half."

In that era before free agency, when teams stayed intact for the most part over several years, the Giants believed they were poised to win several titles. But the players' strike blew apart the 1987 season. The following year, the Giants had to beat the Jets in the season finale to win their division. But Al Toon caught a touchdown pass with 37 seconds remaining, for a 27–21 victory. That night the Rams beat the 49ers—who else?—which knocked the Giants out of the playoffs. Many of the Giants from that era believe the 1989 team was their best. They won the NFC East with a 12–4 record and earned a first-round bye. But the Giants lost a home divisional playoff game in overtime to the Rams when Flipper Anderson caught a touchdown pass from Jim Everett and ran directly up the tunnel to the locker room.

"I get disappointed by '88," Simms said. "That was a funny team. We were going to be so dangerous in the playoffs, and we lost that game to the Jets that we had no reason losing. And of course '89 . . . we were so much better than the Rams in that playoff game. That was probably the worst defeat of my career. For Bill and me, no question, it was our worst game ever together. I can honestly say it was one of the few times I felt the pressure of trying to win a game. We were so much more physical and dominant, it's still incredible we lost that game."

The 1990 Giants won their first ten games. So did the 49ers. Both teams lost game number 11 before the Giants traveled to San Francisco for a Monday night game. The Niners won an intense, riveting contest 7–3. On December 15 the Giants lost for the third time in four games, 17–13, to the Buffalo Bills. More significantly, Simms suffered a broken foot that would sideline him for the remainder of the season.

Parcells turned to Jeff Hostetler, who had been with the Giants since 1984, but had started only three games. Hostetler led the Giants to victories in their final two regular season games and a rout of Chicago in an NFC divisional playoff game. That put the Giants in the NFC Championship Game in San Francisco, the final battle in the classic rivalry. The 49ers had finished with a record of 14–2 and were the two-time defending Super Bowl champions. The talk of a "three-peat" was on the lips of everyone in the Bay Area. The Niners were so confident of victory that they spent $30,000 on furniture, office supplies, and phone lines in a hotel in Tampa, the site of Super Bowl XXV.

The money was wasted. The Giants won a game for the ages as Matt Bahr's 42-yard field goal, his fifth of the game, came as time expired and clinched a breathtaking 15–13 victory. "That was probably the greatest game I ever coached," Parcells said. "Think about who was playing in that game, on our side and their side. It was just a tremendous thing. Jerry Markbreit told me it was the greatest game he ever refereed, and he did 467 of them. That's the best one I was ever at. I love it. That's one I really think about."

Hostetler completed 15 of 27 passes for 176 yards, and the Giants rushed for 152 yards. But two big fourth-quarter plays won the game. With the Giants trailing 13–9, linebacker Gary Reasons

Coach Bill Parcells raises the Vince Lombardi Trophy after the Giants defeat Buffalo in Super Bowl XXV.

caught a snap on a fake punt and ran 30 yards to San Francisco's 24 yard line. The up-back who was blocking for Sean Landeta, Reasons noticed that the 49ers had just ten men on the field. Bill Romanowski had been knocked groggy and didn't run onto the field with the punt return team. Reasons turned to the sidelines and yelled "Arapahoe!," the Giants' fake punt call: a run, a pass, a hit on the enemy. He then made the play that set up Bahr's fourth field goal.

On the 49ers ensuing drive, Erik Howard forced a fumble by Roger Craig that was recovered by Taylor at the Giants 43 yard line. Hostetler completed passes of 19 yards to Bavaro and 13 yards to Stephen Baker to set up the winning field goal.

The incredible victory put the Giants in Super Bowl XXV against the Buffalo Bills, a high-scoring outfit that used a high-speed, no-huddle attack that had just scored 51 points in the AFC title game against Oakland. But the Giants owned the ball for a Super Bowl record 40 minutes 33 seconds and scored the winning points on Bahr's 21-yard field goal midway through the fourth period. But the victory wasn't secure until Buffalo's Scott Norwood pushed a 47-yard field-goal attempt wide right in the final seconds.

"It was supposed to be the Neanderthals against the new wave and all that crap," Parcells said. "We were pretty good underdogs. Some people in New York were picking us to lose by four or five touchdowns. Then they said we were lucky to win because he missed the kick. I feel just the opposite. I feel like we dominated that game. We held the ball for forty-one minutes. If we had lost that game, it would have been a shame. I think we outplayed them. We played smart football. It was a great reflection on the players. We had good, long drives in that game executed to perfection—two of them in a row, one right near the half, one in the third quarter. It was great. It was a great feeling. That was a very satisfying win right there."

The second Super Bowl victory validated Parcells's coaching genius. He won the title twice in five seasons, with two vastly different teams. Only seven players started for the Giants in both Super Bowls. Then, on May 15, 1991, Parcells shocked the world in announcing his resignation as the coach of the Giants, signaling the end of the most successful era in Giants history.

The Coaches

Miami University in Oxford, Ohio, has long been known in sports circles as the "Cradle of Coaches." The list of Miami graduates who became great football coaches includes Earl H. (Red) Blaik, Woody Hayes, Ara Parseghian, Bo Schembechler, Weeb Ewbank, Paul Brown, and many others. But no NFL team has earned a similar designation, though the Giants are certainly worthy. The cast of coaches who have worked for the franchise, either as the head coach or as assistants, is arguably more impressive than any other team in the league.

The register of head coaches includes Steve Owen, a member of the Pro Football Hall of Fame; Bill Parcells, a two-time Super Bowl winner and eleventh on the NFL's career victory list; Dan Reeves, the seventh-winningest coach in league history; Jim Lee Howell; Tom Coughlin; Jim Fassel; and Ray Perkins.

The lineup of assistant coaches is even more striking. It begins with Vince Lombardi and Tom Landry, who were Howell's top assistants in the 1950s. Both are in the Pro Football Hall of Fame. Lombardi, who coached the offense, is regarded by many as the greatest coach in professional team sports history. He coached the Green Bay Packers for ten years and won five championships in seven seasons, including victories in the first two Super Bowls. Landry coached the Dallas Cowboys for the first twenty-nine years of their existence and won two of the five Super Bowls to which he led his team.

The tradition of accomplished assistant coaches continues today. Almost a quarter of the current NFL head coaches are former Giants aides. The list includes five one-time defensive coordinators: Parcells; Bill Belichick, who has won three Super Bowls with the New England Patriots; Marty Schottenheimer, who is ninth on the career victory list; John Fox, who led the Carolina Panthers to Super Bowl XXXVIII against Belichick's Patriots; and Mike Nolan, the new coach of the San Francisco 49ers. The other former assistants now in top jobs are: Coughlin, the Giants' receivers coach from 1988 to 1990, who led the Jacksonville Jaguars to four playoff berths in their first five seasons, an NFL first; and Romeo Crennel, a special teams and defensive line coach from 1981 to 1992, who is the new head man in Cleveland.

The tradition of great coaches began with Owen, who won 153 games from 1931 to 1953, a franchise record, and was elected to the Hall of Fame in 1966. "He was a father figure to all the players out here," Wellington Mara said. "And he wasn't afraid to change things." Owen was the visionary behind the A formation on offense and the Umbrella defense. He had a reputation as being a rugged, hard-nosed coach, but Mara said, "His bark was much worse than his bite. One time he was saying something and my brother Jack said to him, 'Steve, where do you bury your dead?'"

After the Giants went 3–9 in 1953, the Maras decided to change coaches, and Owen's long reign ended. The new man was Howell, who wisely hired Lombardi and Landry, the two best coaches to share time on the same sideline in history. "All I have to do with these guys around is check curfews and pump up footballs," Howell said. "Tom and Vince take care of the rest."

Landry, who was a player-coach for two years, was a brilliant defensive strategist who coolly put his players in the best positions to succeed. Lombardi was equally as astute, though his temperament was far more fiery.

Pat Summerall joined the team in 1958. In addition to being the kicker, he was a backup defensive end and tight end. Because he attended the meetings of both units, he was exposed to both Lombardi and Landry. "The thing about Lombardi was his presence and what a great teacher he was," Summerall said. "I remember the first meeting I ever went to with the Giants. People had gotten in at different times, and it was like get-reacquainted

Opening the Umbrella

Head coach Steve Owen unfurled the "Umbrella" defense on October 1, 1950, against Cleveland. The Browns had been absorbed into the NFL after winning four consecutive championships in the All-America Football Conference. In its NFL debut Cleveland had crushed Philadelphia 35–10. Then the Browns routed the Baltimore Colts 31–0. Their next game was against the Giants.

Hall of Fame coach Steve Owen.
New York Giants

"They were on top of the world when we went out to play them," Wellington Mara said. "Steve and [Philadelphia coach] Greasy Neale were rivals but really close friends. Greasy was at that game because the Eagles had an off week. And Steve was so proud to do what his coaching partner and rival hadn't been able to do. And that was the invention of the Umbrella defense, which really was the 5-3 we use today. Steve got to it by dropping both ends off the line of scrimmage. Cleveland always used to get its offense rolling with a quick out to [wide receivers] Mac Speedie or Dante Lavelli, who were great ends. Steve dropped our two defensive ends—Jim Duncan and Ray Poole—so they had that area about 8 to 10 yards from the line of scrimmage, toward the sideline. He counted on [linebacker] John Cannaday to keep Marion Motley under control. And it all worked out."

The Giants won 6–0, handing the Browns their first shutout loss since the franchise began in 1946.

day because everybody was coming back from the off-season. The guys had been out and had a couple of beers and were just happy to see each other. Somebody was trying to call the roll and he couldn't get the guys quiet—there were about one hundred of us in the room. And Lombardi walked in and just cleared his throat and the room got silent. And I said to whoever I was sitting next to, 'Who the hell is that?' And I think it was Don Heinrich, and he said, 'That is Lombardi, and you will know who he is soon enough.' There was an aura about him.

"I will never forget about what a great teacher he was. Repetition was a big part of his teaching. He knew every detail of every step you should take; how long your step should be to keep the pulling guard from stepping on the quarterback's feet. He had such a great, great command of what he was talking about. And Landry to a degree was the same way, but much quieter. Landry's theory was, 'Here is what you are suppose to do, and if you do it, we'll win.' And if you did it, it turned out to be true, you would win. But you never knew where you stood with Landry—he never praised anybody, he never said you did a good job, he never said anything. It was a job and that was what you were supposed to do. And if you did it, you did it without recognition or praise or anything. Lombardi was a little bit different from that. They were both dynamic. You knew that they were both great teachers, but I think the one that left the lasting impression, the really lasting impression, was Lombardi."

Frank Gifford, who was a Pro Bowler on offense and defense at different times in his career, knew both Lombardi and Landry well. "They were polar opposites in demeanor," Gifford said. "I really liked Tom. We were good friends with Tom and his wife,

Alicia. We became friends after I moved to the offensive side of the ball. We lived in the same hotel, the Concourse Plaza. Tom and Alicia liked to play bridge, and my wife Maxine and I liked to play bridge. We spent a lot of time together.

"Lombardi was the teacher. When he put his offense in, it consisted of a 49 sweep, a 47 power, a 41 trap. The other way he had a 29 sweep; a 26 power, which was the halfback off tackle; and a 20, which was a quick trap. That was just about the entire running offense. Each week he would change the blocking assignments according to the defense we anticipated. I recall him saying to Bill Austin, 'Bill, on 49 sweep I want you to drop the right foot, you have to drop the right foot. You have to be moving when you drop the right foot, moving when you drop the foot, moving when you drop the foot. If you don't, the left guard will be on top of you, the left guard will be on top of you if you don't drop the right foot.' You didn't forget it. That's the way he coached. He didn't leave anything to your imagination. Landry was a different type of person who believed in the same things."

Landry began building the 4–3 defense in 1956 around a rookie middle linebacker named Sam Huff. "Lombardi yelled. Landry never did do that," Huff said. "Lombardi cussed. Landry never did do that. He said 'dag-bird.' That's an old Texas expression. One time I went the wrong way. I keyed the quarterback. I just knew what he was going to do. I took my pass drop, and the quarterback threw the ball and I intercepted it. I got the turnover, so I'm happy. I come to the sideline and sit down, and Landry comes over and looked at me and said, 'What do you think you're doing?' I said, 'Tom, I keyed the quarterback and I knew what he was going to do—I got the interception.' He said, 'Sam, you've got to play my defense. You know you took the wrong pass drop. If that fullback comes out of that backfield, and he's going down the field, and the quarterback pumps once and throws, and they get a touchdown, you've got to play the defense that we prepared you for.' I never took the wrong drop again.

"Landry was a perfectionist. And you had to believe in what he was doing. We lived together at the same hotel. I lived upstairs, and he'd call me and say, 'What are you doing?' 'Well, I'm watching television, Tom.' 'C'mon up and let's look at some film.' He was teaching me to play middle linebacker, because I never played linebacker before. I played both ways in college— offensive and defensive lineman. I never played linebacker. But when he put me there, I could see everything. He told me when I first started, 'I never want you to do anything in this defense you think you can't do.'"

Lombardi and Landry eventually became two of the very best head coaches in NFL history—but not with the Giants. Mara would have liked to have kept them. But Lombardi got an offer to coach Green Bay prior to the 1959 season. He loved his native New York, but he also wanted to be a head coach. The next year Howell surprised everyone by resigning. Landry was still on the staff, but he wouldn't have stayed even if ownership of the Empire State Building had been included in his contract.

"I called Tom in and offered him the job," Mara said. "He said he was leaving the next day and had an appointment in Texas [it was actually with the Houston franchise of the new American Football League]. And I couldn't talk him out of it. He said, 'I want to go back to Texas.' He also said one very interesting thing. He said, 'I know I can do the job. I know what it takes to win now. I've learned that from Lombardi.'

"And as quick as he left, I called up Tex Schramm, because the Dallas Cowboys were being formed. I didn't want to see Tom go to the other league. So I call up Tex and gave Landry a big recommendation to him. I said, 'Look, he wants to coach in Texas, you better get him.'"

After Landry rebuffed his advances, Mara investigated the possibility of Lombardi returning to the Giants. "When the Packers came to me to ask for permission to talk to Vinny, I said yes, but I said I want one thing: I want to be free to bring him back if we ever want him," Mara said. "At that time, we had no thought that we would ever lose Howell. And they very willingly agreed because it was probably the farthest thing from their thoughts that that would be a problem.

"I tried to get Lombardi back, but he felt he would be running out on the people in Green Bay. I think also he knew he was making himself a great team, and he didn't want to lose it."

Unable to secure his first two choices, Mara turned to Allie Sherman, who had been an offensive coach under Owen. Sherman led the Giants to three consecutive championship games (1961–63), but lost all three.

The next head coach to make a significant impact on the Giants was Ray Perkins. He was hired in 1979 by George Young to lead the Giants out of the wilderness after fifteen years worth of poor performances. Perkins was demanding, stern, and unyielding. The phrase frequently used about Perkins is that he made it "uncomfortable to lose."

"My second camp under Ray Perkins was probably the

toughest four or five weeks I ever endured in pro football," Phil Simms said. "It was physically and mentally as hard as it ever got for me in my fifteen years—and I was a damn quarterback. I did more running—this is no exaggeration—after practice in one week in that training camp than most teams do in a whole season now. There were days when I said, 'I don't think I can make it.' Guys would pass out on the field. There were days when we would have five or six in a day taken away in ambulances because they were dehydrating or overheating on the field. If that happened now, they'd have to stop practice for a week."

Simms recalled a players-only meeting in which center Jim Clack was chosen to speak to Perkins and tell him if things didn't change, the players would walk out. That was not a good idea. "In 1980 we played the Pittsburgh Steelers on a Saturday night and just got destroyed," Simms said. "I'm not sure if we scrimmaged the next day or the next practice after the game on Monday. I think we ran 42 plays, and 40 of them were runs, and it was first defense against first offense. Nobody substituted. And it was live. In that one practice we did more hitting than a lot of teams do in a whole year. Teams never hit like that.

"I'll never forget, when the practice was over, we were all sitting in the auditorium waiting for our night meeting. Not one player said anything. You could hear a pin drop. Perkins dropped his yellow notebook on the podium and said, 'Men, I don't care if every one of you leaves. I'll go out and get me forty-five new guys and we'll play with them. So if you don't like the way I'm doing things, tough. Leave. I don't care. I don't care who you are or what you play.' So I said to myself, 'Okay, things aren't going to change around here.'"

Calling the Roll

Here are the head coaches of the Giants and each one's overall record (including postseason):

Years	Name	Record
1925	Bob Folwell	8–4–0
1926	Joe Alexander	8–4–1
1927–28	Earl Potteiger	15–8–3
1929–30	LeRoy Andrews*	24–5–1
1930	Benny Friedman/ Steve Owen	2–0–0
1931–53	Steve Owen	153–108–17
1954–60	Jim Lee Howell	55–29–4
1961–68	Allie Sherman	57–54–4
1969–73	Alex Webster	29–40–1
1974–76	Bill Arnsparger**	7–28–0
1976–78	John McVay	14–23–0
1979–82	Ray Perkins	24–5–0
1983–90	Bill Parcells	82–52–1
1991–92	Ray Handley	14–18–0
1993–96	Dan Reeves	32–34–0
1997–2003	Jim Fassel	60–56–1
2004	Tom Coughlin	6–10–0

* Released after 15 games in 1930.

** Released after 7 games in 1976.

Perkins drove the Giants to a playoff berth in 1981, their first in eighteen years. But the next year Alabama coach Bear Bryant retired, and Perkins had the opportunity to realize the dream of coaching at his alma mater. When he left, Young promoted defensive coordinator Bill Parcells.

Today Parcells is acknowledged as one of the finest coaches in NFL history. He is also known as a master motivator who drives his players hard. "Bill has always been my favorite coach," Hall of Fame linebacker Lawrence Taylor said. "He took me and he molded me and he made me into a player. My ability had something to do with that. I think what Bill Parcells brought to the table was tremendous as far as I was concerned."

Parcells could push Taylor's buttons to get him to perform better. When L. T. was a rookie, Parcells repeatedly ran tape of Hugh Green, a linebacker who was taken five picks after Taylor in the 1981 NFL draft. "I'd say, 'There's that 53—who is that 53?'" Parcells said. "'Is that the same guy in all these plays? . . . Look at this guy, he's great.' Finally after about three weeks, Taylor couldn't take it anymore. He said, 'Why didn't you draft that son of a bitch if you love him so much?' And everybody started laughing. Because they knew I was giving it to him. He had an easy buzzer. You could get him."

Years later—Parcells thinks it was 1989—Parcells approached Taylor and said, "Did you change your name?" Taylor looked at Parcells as if he had two heads. Parcells said, "The press keeps asking me, 'What's the matter with Taylor?' I'm going to change your name to that: 'What's the matter with?'" Taylor went out and pulverized the opposition that week.

In the 1986 Monday night victory in San Francisco, the Giants rushed for 13 yards. Before the teams met in a playoff game five weeks later, Parcells burst into an offensive line meeting and asked, "Is this the meeting of Club 13?" The Giants rushed for 216 yards in a 49–3 rout.

Parcells, however, worked no one like Simms. The coach was all over his quarterback each and every day of the season. "He was vicious," Simms said. "I'd walk out of the locker room to go to practice some days, and I'd walk by him and he'd say, 'Hey, Simms, do you think you can complete a couple of passes today in practice? What did you hit yesterday, like 5 for 30? I couldn't even sleep last night because you were so bad. I was tossing and turning and my wife said, "What's the matter, Bill?" and I said, "My quarterback can't complete a pass." Can I get some sleep?' Of course it was much saltier than that. Wow. I'd come out of the locker room and break into cold sores immediately because of nerves. [Receivers coach] Pat Hodgson would hear it and he couldn't help but laugh. Pat would go, 'I'll go warn the receivers it might be coming a little hard today.'

"If I didn't throw to the right guy—if I threw the ball to the back in the flat—he'd yell and scream, 'What's the matter, are you worried about your little pass completion percentage? I can run the sweep for 4 yards. I need some yards, throw it and quit worrying about your stupid rating.' It was rough. He'd stick his head in the huddle and stand behind me in practice, 'There he is, throw it.' Who? What? I'd heave it right into the middle of everything. 'Not him, dammit.'"

Simms is a voracious reader, so he knows a great deal about Lombardi. And when he reads about Lombardi, he can't help but think of Parcells. "Kill them during the week, love them in the game," Simms said. "Right before the game say, 'You guys are the best, there's nobody like you, there's no way you can lose, you're great.' That was how Lombardi treated his guys, too."

Parcells tolerated, even encouraged, loud discourse with his players. "Simms dared to answer back to Coach Parcells, and that's what endeared him to Parcells," Wellington Mara said. "Bill knew he couldn't bully him. Phil would give it right back to him, and Bill appreciated that."

"A lot of players yelled at Bill: Lawrence, Jim Burt, [Bart] Oates—a lot of guys talked back," Simms said. "Maurice Carthon, oh my God, they used to say things to each other and I'd say, 'Wow.' It's pretty unique for a coach to let his players do that. He liked it. He'd come up to me after an argument and say, 'Man, that was a good one. You really hated me, didn't you?' It's strange when you get that."

It was unusual, but it was effective. Parcells was 85–52–1 in eight seasons as the coach of the Giants (including playoffs). But when he resigned in May of 1991, the system fell apart. After two years of chaos under Ray Handley, Reeves was brought in after he was fired by the Denver Broncos.

In 1993, Reeves's first year as coach, the Giants and Cowboys were 11–4 as they headed into the season finale in Giants Stadium. The winner would get home-field advantage throughout the playoffs, while the loser would drop to a wild card. After four periods the game was tied at 13–13.

"I can remember the coin toss for overtime like it was yesterday," Simms said. "I stood right next to Bart Oates and he said, 'What do you think?' I said, 'If we win this overtime, we're going to go to the Super Bowl. If we lose, we have no chance.' I remember seeing his face. I knew as a wild card we would have to beat

the 49ers and the Cowboys on the road. We had no chance." Simms was correct. After a wild victory over Minnesota, the Giants were crushed 44–3 in San Francisco.

Reeves left after the 1996 season and was replaced by Fassel, who led the Giants to a division title his first year and an NFC title in 2000. Coughlin was hired on January 6, 2004, and with Eli Manning at quarterback, he figures to guide the Giants to much success in the coming years.

The Guarantee

Jim Fassel was widely assumed to be on the coaching hot seat before the Giants opened their 2000 season. Three years earlier, Fassel, a former offensive coordinator who had been a Giants' assistant in 1991 and 1992, had revived a team that had sputtered the previous two seasons under Dan Reeves. In his first season Fassel had earned much capital by leading the Giants to a 10–5–1 record and a surprise NFC East championship.

But much of that capital had been spent when the Giants fell to 8–8 and then 7–9 in the next two years. With fans, the media, and the front office growing restless, Fassel likely needed to return to the playoffs in 2000 to keep his job. His job security was enhanced when the Giants started 7–2. Then the defending Super Bowl–champion St. Louis Rams invaded New Jersey. They easily defeated the Giants, 38–24.

The following week was even worse for the Giants. They fell behind a mediocre Detroit Lions team 28–0 on their way to a 31–21 loss. In those eight days the heat on Fassel went from a gentle simmer to full boil. To critics and skeptics, he had one foot out the door. But instead of retreating, Fassel came out swinging, in the grand New York tradition of Joe Namath, Mark Messier, and Patrick Ewing. Three days after the Detroit debacle, at his regular Wednesday news conference, a defiant Fassel stunned everyone by guaranteeing that the Giants would make the playoffs. Not only did he not try to diffuse the pressure on him, Fassel willingly added to it. "Get off my coaches' backs, get off the players' backs," Fassel said. "I'm responsible for the whole thing. I'll take control of the whole thing right now. I'm redefining where we're going." Moments later, Fassel declared, "This team is going to the playoffs."

His shocking prediction proved to be correct, and then some. The Giants won their last five regular-season games and two post-season games, including a 41–0 rout of Minnesota in the NFC Championship Game, and played in Super Bowl XXXV. They lost to the Baltimore Ravens, the team, ironically, that now employs Fassel as offensive coordinator. But Fassel's guarantee set the stage for one of the most memorable seasons in Giants' history.

"By doing what he did, he put himself in a no-lose situation," said running back Tiki Barber, who has always been a strong Fassel supporter. "If we don't make the playoffs, he's going to be fired anyway. If we do make the playoffs, he's going to look like a genius. It was a genius move. You can't argue with anything that he did. He knew how to manipulate us to play better, and that's what he did."

"I think what it did for him and his coaching staff is they just turned it up a notch and decided, 'All right, we are going to get into our playoff mode right now,'" cornerback Jason Sehorn said. "Everything just kind of changed from there—the attitude of the players and of the coaches. From that point on everything was done the way he wanted it done, right on through."

The loss to Detroit was one of the team's sloppiest games in Fassel's seven years as coach. The Giants had 4 turnovers, rushed for only 53 yards, and allowed Desmond Howard to gain 145 yards on punt and kickoff returns, including a 50-yard punt return that set up a touchdown.

On a solitary drive after the game, Fassel thought long and hard about how he could reverse the team's slump. He said little to his family when he arrived home. The following day, he made a move that got everyone's attention, releasing special teams performer Bashir Levingston, twenty-four hours after his holding penalty negated Barber's 67-yard punt return and after he fumbled away a kickoff. Levingston had been special teams MVP in 1999.

"That sent a signal in the locker room—'If he'll cut him, he'll cut anybody,'" Fassel said. "After our team meeting that day, I told twelve guys I wanted to meet them in another room. They were primarily our core special teams players. This was the fun part; I think this signaled the change as much as anything. I told them I

Former head coach Jim Fassel on the sideline prior to the kickoff of Super Bowl XXXV.

was going to cut two of them a week, every week, if we didn't play better on special teams. I don't care if we win the game. If we don't play better on special teams, two of you are going to go out the door. I don't care who they are. But two of you are going to go out the door. And you're in competition with the guys on your team.

"I remember Brandon Short and Jack Golden walked out of that meeting and went straight to Jessie Armstead. They said, 'Did you hear what he told us in that meeting? He's going to cut two of us every week if we don't play better.' Jessie said, 'He cut the special teams MVP from a year ago, you guys are two rookies, I don't think he gives a damn about you two guys. You guys better play better.'"

But Fassel knew he needed to do more. He still had confidence in his team and himself. It didn't take long for him to become convinced that a guarantee was the correct path to take. That afternoon in the Giants Stadium media room, Fassel made one of the most metaphorically filled speeches anyone had ever heard. He started by telling reporters, "Let me define some things right now with you guys, exactly what my approach is with this football team."

Fassel then assumed a wide variety of roles as he made his way through the speech. He was a train conductor. ("I'm driving the train and all we've got to do is listen and follow along.") He was a bus driver. ("I'm driving the bus. Follow along. I don't want any variation of what I'm saying. I'll take full responsibility—the offense, the defense, special teams, whether we win, whether we lose.") He was a jockey. ("This is a race horse and we're coming around the far turn and I see the finish line. I want no ambiguity on where we're going to go. I'm going to define it completely.") He was a target. ("If you've got the crosshairs, if you've got the laser, you can put it right on my chest. I'll take full responsibility.")

And he was a gambler. ("I'm raising the stakes right now. If this is a poker game, I'm shoving my chips to the middle of the table. I'm raising the ante. Anybody that wants in, gets in. Anybody that wants out can get out.")

"I didn't want anybody dictating to us what was going to happen," Fassel said. "I didn't want anyone dictating to me. There was a lot of speculation in the media at the time that I should fire Larry MacDuff as special teams coach. That was permeating everywhere. The team couldn't do this and it couldn't do that, and everything started to turn negative. I thought there was too much speculation on things, I thought it was going to become a distraction to the team, I thought I needed to send a message to everybody—everybody around the organization, the fans, the media, everyone, as to what our direction was. I wanted to get the pressure off everybody else, off the players, off the coaches, off everybody, and put it on my back, which is where it was going to go anyhow.

"What happened from then on—people immediately forgot we had gotten beat by the Rams and Detroit. The focus shifted to the guarantee and how stupid I was to do that."

Fassel said he didn't take the podium that day with a prepared speech. The conductor, the bus driver, and the poker player just appeared as he was speaking. "All those metaphors were just rolling out of me," Fassel said. "I did not write one down. They were things I had used throughout my life in my frame of reference. I talked to myself constantly, but I never wrote anything down, and I never rehearsed anything. Those are things that crossed my mind at different times. I didn't want to sound angry. I just wanted to say, this is what we're going to do. If you don't like it, get the hell out of the way."

Fassel never told the players about the guarantee. They heard about it from the media, whose members were eager to gauge the team's reaction to Fassel's bold declaration. "That speech was like the 'Play of the Day' for three months straight," defensive end Michael Strahan said. "When he did that, we were under a lot of scrutiny. We had lost that game to Detroit that we should have won. I think there was a lot of pressure on everybody. But when he stepped up and did that, it was as if he told us as players, 'I'm putting it on my back.' We appreciated him taking the pressure off of us. So we wanted to go perform for him."

That's exactly what they did. Four days after the guarantee, the Giants were in Arizona, where they crushed the Cardinals, 31–7. The following week they were in Washington and squeaked out a 9–7 victory that put them in control of the NFC East race. "Probably one of the tough, hard-nosed games we played was at Washington," Fassel said. "It was a tough-assed game and that one as much as anything turned it around. I felt after that game we were going in the right direction. Arizona was fine, but we needed a tough, hard-nosed game to win on the road to prove to ourselves that we were tough enough."

The Giants returned home to rout Pittsburgh 30–10. A come-from-behind 17–13 victory in Dallas clinched the division title. They ended the regular season with a 28–25 victory over Jacksonville that guaranteed home-field advantage throughout the playoffs. The regular-season record after the guarantee: 5–0.

"When you get on a roll like that it's fun, because you can't make yourself lose," Barber said. "When things go bad, somehow, someone finds a way to make it better. It's not always the same guy—it wasn't always [quarterback] Kerry Collins or Michael or

Jessie. It was somebody. On that team everyone had the mentality, 'Why not me? I'll make a play today.' And it always got done."

"The focus of everybody that year was amazing," Strahan said. "First of all, we were healthy. Secondly, we had chemistry. Third, we didn't make a lot of mistakes. And our star players played like stars every week. That's what did it for us."

The Giants' first playoff game was against their ancient division foes, the Eagles. They had not lost to Philadelphia since 1996, their two victories that season stretching their winning streak to eight games. But everyone knew number nine would be the most difficult. "That was the highest-pressure game I ever coached as the Giants' head coach," Fassel said. "The most pressure. We had beaten them eight straight times, we had home-field advantage through the playoffs, so we were in prime position. But I knew they had a good team. And I knew all of our games with them were hard fought. If we let them come in as a wild-card team from our own division after we had beaten them eight straight times, if my team overlooks them, we're in trouble. And you know Philly would be ticked. If we let them beat us, it's going to be embarrassing, because the road to the Super Bowl is coming through New York. That would have been bad. I felt like that, and I felt like the whole staff felt like that."

The Giants won 20–10, but they did not score an offensive touchdown. Ron Dixon returned the opening kickoff 97 yards, Brad Daluiso kicked 2 field goals, and Sehorn made one of the most spectacular plays in the history of Giants Stadium to return an interception 32 yards for a score. Donovan McNabb tried to hit Torrance Small near the right sideline. Sehorn dove for the ball and batted it up in the air, rolled over, then somehow caught the ball after righting himself. He then raced untouched to the end zone, sending the towel-waving fans into delirium. In essence Sehorn tapped the ball to himself, flipped over, caught it, and ran.

"As I dove for it, I had my hands on it, and my elbow hit the ground, and it kind of popped up," Sehorn said. "I was still in a position where I saw it. From then on it was more reflex and reaction. It wasn't anything planned, but more, 'Hey, there's the ball.' Then I kind of tapped it up. You know those footballs and the way they bounce. I tapped it and it went straight up. It could have gone left, right, out of bounds. But it went straight up, and all of a sudden I just instinctively just got up, and I just took off for the end zone. It was just one of those plays where everything has to work perfectly. I think of Franco Harris's play against the Raiders [the famed "Immaculate Reception" in 1972]. If that ball would have bounced off his helmet and went straight to the ground, he would have never had a chance to catch that ball. But sometimes that ball, when you tip it around, or it hits things, it just bounces perfectly. And this was one of those things when that thing just bounced perfectly—straight up, and when I tipped it, it went up. And then the best part about it was the Eagles challenged it, so we watched it five different times on the big screen as they reviewed it. Then I said, 'Wow, it's kind of cool.' It looked good on a Jumbotron. Then I realized that it was something special."

In the NFC Championship game, the Giants faced the Minnesota Vikings, a high-scoring outfit whose lethal aerial attack featured quarterback Daunte Culpepper and wide receiver Randy Moss. In the days leading up to the game, Fassel lectured everyone outside of the team about running the football, controlling the clock, and keeping the offense of the Vikings off the

working on our passing game. We had the complete counter-game-plan to what everyone thought we were going to do. From the first snap in the game, Sean proved to be very prophetic."

Giants Stadium was alive that day with a record crowd of 79,310, most of them waving white towels. It was thirty-five degrees and the grass field was slippery—miserable conditions for a team like the Vikings, which plays its home games in an antiseptic dome. "When you walked out the tunnel and saw that, saw the energy, it was over," Strahan said. "I'm glad we were at home with that crowd, because on the road with that type of crowd and that type of response, it would have been next to impossible to win."

It was for the Vikings. They trailed 14–0 just 2:13 into the game. By halftime it was 34–0, and the Giants had 338 passing yards, making Payton's prophecy come true. The final was 41–0. The Giants outgained Minnesota, 518–114, had 31 first downs to 9 for the Vikings, and owned the ball for a remarkable 42:22. Sehorn covered Moss all afternoon and held him to 2 catches for 18 yards.

Two weeks later, the season ended on a sour note with a 34–7 loss to Baltimore in Super Bowl XXXV. "They were incredible on defense," Fassel said. "We were manhandled up front."

Although the ending left a bad taste in everyone's mouth, the players who made good on Fassel's guarantee recall that season fondly. "The camaraderie that year was unlike any other year I've ever had," Strahan said. "It was special. It has to be in order to go that far. You have to be unselfish. That was definitely a special year."

"It was a great year," Barber said. "It was a great experience with a bunch of great guys, a great coach. We would have liked to finish it the right way, but we didn't. Which is why I'm more determined to get there before I have to retire."

The
Players

The day before Super Bowl XXXIX was
played in Jacksonville, the big news in pro
football circles was the election of Dan
Marino and Steve Young to the Pro Football
Hall of Fame. The two great quarterbacks
were elected in their first year of eligibility.

Not quite as newsworthy was the selection to the Hall of Benny Friedman, who
played for the Giants from 1929 to 1931. Pro
football's first great passer, Friedman played

in the NFL from 1927 to 1934. As a rookie with the Cleveland Bulldogs, he threw an NFL-record 11 touchdown passes. Two years later, he set another mark when he passed for 20 scores for the Giants. His 66 career touchdown passes was an NFL record until Hall of Famer Arnie Herber surpassed him in 1944, the first of his two seasons with the Giants. "He towered over his contemporaries," Wellington Mara said, "and set the stage of the development of the passing game we see today."

Friedman's acquisition by the Giants is part of NFL lore. Team owner Tim Mara so coveted Friedman that he purchased the Detroit Wolverines, the team Friedman played for in 1928. Mara then disbanded the Wolverines franchise but kept Friedman.

In 1930 Friedman was also the Giants head coach, along with Steve Owen, for the final two games. Owen went on to coach the Giants through the 1953 season. Friedman played one more season for the Giants, then finished his career with a three-year stint with the Brooklyn Dodgers.

Friedman is the twenty-eighth member of the Hall with a connection to the Giants. The group includes owners (both Maras), coaches (Steve Owen, Vince Lombardi, Tom Landry), players who spent their entire careers with the Giants (Lawrence Taylor, Frank Gifford, Roosevelt Brown), and players who were with the franchise for as little as one season (Don Maynard, Fran Tarkenton, and Larry Csonka). The team has also had dozens of excellent players who are not enshrined in the Hall, such Phil Simms, Harry Carson, and Alex Webster.

In their long and glorious history, the Giants have employed players from Abrams (Bobby, a linebacker from 1990 to 1992) to Zyntell (Jim, a guard who played in 1933). It's quite possible they have featured more great and/or colorful players than any other franchise. Many, like Friedman, took somewhat bizarre routes just to join the team.

One was Hall of Famer Mel Hein, who was a great center for fifteen seasons, a record of team service matched only by Simms. Hein played collegiate ball at Washington State, so the Giants sent him a contract in the mail for the unheard of sum of $5,000 for the 1931 season. By the time it arrived, Hein had already signed and returned a contract to Providence, where the owner of the Washington Redskins, George Preston Marshall, kept his office. But Hein wanted to play for the Giants, so he called Tim Mara and asked him if it was possible to break his contract with Marshall.

Acting on Mara's suggestion, Hein sent a telegram to the Providence postmaster, asking him to return the letter. To his amazement that's exactly what happened, and the Giants got Hein, who was a sixty-minute player virtually every time he suited up in his fifteen-year career. Turns out the Giants had help. The Providence postmaster was Bill Halloran, who happened to love football. He gave the Giants a big assist in the procurement of Hein.

All these years later, Wellington Mara still has high praise for Hein's skill and contributions to the team. "You can't compare players from one era to another era," Mara said. "All you can do is say how they compared with other players in their own era. And I would say Mel Hein would have been the greatest Giant, because he was so superior to the other players of his era.

"He was not effusive. He really led by example more than anything. He was universally called 'Pappy.' He was a guy you'd know would always be there. I think he was impervious to injuries. The first time he ever had to call time out, he got kicked in the nose by one of our own players in a pileup. That was very, very late in his career. He was extraordinarily tough, but you didn't get the impression of toughness from him. I don't think he ever lifted a weight in his life, but he had tremendous strength. Anything you would want a player to have, he had. He was about 6' 2" or 6' 3" and 225 pounds. That wouldn't be big today. But compared to the players of his era, he towered over them."

Y. A. Tittle also had an unusual arrival when he joined the team in a trade prior to the 1961 season. Tittle, a Hall of Famer, played three seasons for Baltimore and ten for San Francisco when he found himself battling John Brodie for the 49ers starting quarterback job. The talk in San Francisco was that perhaps Tittle should retire and let Brodie take over. But Tittle was determined to keep his job and planned to prove he should when the Giants and 49ers met in the 1961 preseason opener in Portland.

"There was a lot of trade talk before the game," Tittle said. "John Brodie was going to play the first half, and I was going to play the second half. Red Hickey, our coach, had come up with a new formation that involved a 'Shotgun' offense. He was running reverses and double reverses and running all kinds of wide-open things with the running backs and the quarterbacks that I wasn't accustomed to. Brodie opened up against that famed New York Giant defense of Andy Robustelli and Sam Huff, and they just killed him—I mean killed him. I think the score was 21–0 at halftime. I didn't want to pull against my team, but I was so happy, because Brodie got mutilated and I was going to come in for the second half and play in the old-fashioned T formation. And I was trying to save my job.

"I went out there in the second half, and I never had it better in my life. Never—not in high school, not in college. I threw thirty-some-odd passes and I was never touched. One time Robustelli rushed through and hit me and knocked me down, then picked me up and brushed me off. 'Are you okay?' he asked me. 'What do you mean, am I okay?' I never had a defensive end ask me that question before. I said, 'No problem.' I was ripping them apart. One touchdown, two touchdowns, three touchdowns. Sam Huff ripped on through, had a clean shot at me, and at the last second, he'd veer off."

The Giants won the game 21–20, but that was incidental to Tittle, who thought he had played well enough to put Brodie back on the bench—"back where he belonged," Tittle said. Tittle soon learned that Brodie was going nowhere, but he was.

"I'm walking back to the locker room, and here comes Sam Huff," Tittle said. "He says, 'Y. A., I want to be the first to congratulate you. Our coach, Allie Sherman, told us right before the game that he had traded for you, and if anybody touched you, it would cost them a thousand dollars.' I tried using that story sometimes later on in my career when some of these guys were roughing me up. I'd say, 'I hear I'm being traded to you.'"

Sherman had issued a stern warning to his players before the game: Anyone who messes with Tittle will suffer dire consequences. "I will never forget the looks on the faces of those guys," Sherman said. "I said, 'He is going to be playing against us, but tomorrow morning he belongs to us. The first guy that puts a tough piece of leather on him, you are out of here.' They got a big chuckle out of that. He was a great player for us." Tittle played four seasons for the Giants and led them to the NFL Championship Game in 1961, 1962, and 1963.

Roosevelt Brown, who passed away in 2004, spent fifty years in the organization as a player, coach, and scout. He was selected in the twenty-seventh round of the 1953 draft out of Morgan State. "It was getting pretty skimpy," Mara said. "Ray Walsh and I were looking through All-America teams, and we came to the All-America team of the *Pittsburgh Courier* [once the country's most widely circulated African-American newspaper]. He was on that team. We read about his size and everything they said about him, so we drafted him.

"Ed Kolman was our line coach at the time. He was really a great line coach, and he took an immediate liking to Rosie because he could see that he was someone who was so sincere and so willing to work. No one knew how old Rosie was. He just had the ideal build and he could run. Rosie played on special teams, he played on the goal-line defense. He did everything. I still think the greatest story about Rosie was the time that he and a big defensive lineman from Pittsburgh got in a fight in Yankee Stadium. Both of them got put out of the game, and after the game the press asked Rosie how the fight started. He said, 'The fight started when [Ben] McGee hit me back.' "

His teammates were particularly fond of Brown. "I have a funny story I like to tell about Rosie," Huff said. "When I was a rookie, I didn't have much money, but I had $10—and he borrowed it from me. He said, 'Do you have any money?' I said, 'I have $10,' and he said, 'Loan it to me.' He never paid me back until I made the team. When I made the team, I said, 'Where's my $10?' He said, 'I'd better pay you, because you made the team. I thought you were going to get cut.' "

"Rosie is a Hall of Fame player, and I wouldn't be in the Hall of Fame if it weren't for him," Gifford said. "Our two favorite plays were 48 pitchout and [Vince] Lombardi's 49 sweep, and Rosie was the key man in all of that. The longest run in my career [79 yards] was on a 48 pitchout against Washington. Rosie made a block at the line of scrimmage. I cut it up, and then I'm running downfield and I look up and I see number 79 [Brown] in front of me, and he wiped out another guy."

Gifford was the Giants first-round draft choice in 1952. When he retired after the 1964 season, Gifford held team records for receptions and total yards. "The first word that comes to my mind when I think of Frank is *smoothness*," Mara said. "He never looked as though he was extending himself, but he always was. He went to the Pro Bowl as a running back, and he went to the Pro Bowl as a defensive back. Obviously, he had to be one of the great all-timers. He's been a very good friend of mine for years and years, ever since he played."

Gifford missed the 1961 season after absorbing a crushing hit from Philadelphia linebacker Chuck Bednarik the previous season. "I could have played in '61," Gifford said. "All that stuff about me being knocked out of the game—I was fine. I passed every test they gave me. But I had played nine years, I had three kids, and I was working for WCBS-TV, doing the local sports news. And I knew they wanted to develop me. I stayed out that year in 1961, and everything worked great for me. I was doing the early news, doing specials, and I had a network radio show. I was making more money than I ever made playing football, so that wasn't the issue. But I really missed playing." So he played for three more seasons.

Hall of Fame Giants

Here are the Giants players, coaches, and executives who have been inducted into the Pro Football Hall of Fame. (Players with an asterisk by their name played a major portion of their careers in New York. The others played a minor portion with the club.) With seventeen primary members in the Hall, the Giants trail only the Chicago Bears (26) and the Green Bay Packers (20) among all teams in NFL history.

Name	Year Inducted	Years with Giants
Morris (Red) Badgro*	1981	1930–35
Roosevelt Brown*	1975	1953–65
Larry Csonka	1987	1976–78
Ray Flaherty	1976	1928–29, 1931–35
Benny Friedman*	2005	1929–31
Frank Gifford*	1977	1952–60, 1962–64
Joe Guyon	1966	1927
Mel Hein*	1963	1931–45
Wilbur (Pete) Henry	1963	1927
Arnie Herber	1966	1944–45

Two Giants greats of more-recent vintage, Phil Simms and Lawrence Taylor, were first-round draft choices. Taylor was the second pick of the 1981 draft, a player who revolutionized defensive football in the NFL. No linebacker had ever tormented quarterbacks like L. T., who finished his career with 132.5 sacks.

Name	Year Inducted	Years with Giants
Robert (Cal) Hubbard	1963	1927–28, 1936
Sam Huff*	1982	1956–63
Alphonse (Tuffy) Leemans*	1978	1936–43
Tim Mara*	1963	1925–59
Wellington Mara*	1997	1937–present
Don Maynard	1987	1958
Hugh McElhenny	1970	1963
Steve Owen*	1966	1926–53
Andy Robustelli*	1971	1956–64
Ken Strong*	1967	1933–35, 1939, 1944–47
Fran Tarkenton*	1986	1967–71
Lawrence Taylor*	1999	1981–93
Jim Thorpe	1963	1925
Y. A. Tittle*	1971	1961–64
Emlen Tunnell*	1967	1948–58
Arnie Weinmeister*	1984	1950–53

Taylor played in ten consecutive Pro Bowls, was an All-NFL selection nine times, and was the league's MVP in 1986. But Taylor also created controversy off the field, including incurring a four-game suspension at the start of the 1988 season for violating the NFL's substance abuse policy. Because of that, he was unsure if enough Hall of Fame selectors would vote for him when he became eligible in 1999.

"He called me up and asked me, 'Do you think they're going to keep me out of the Hall of Fame?'" Parcells said. "And I said, 'How in the hell do you think they can keep the best guy that ever played out of the Hall of Fame?' That's what I told him. And that's how I feel about him. How do you keep the best guy that ever played out? You can't do it."

Parcells was the defensive coordinator when Taylor was drafted. He knew instantly that he had a special player, so he tweaked his defense to turn Taylor into a lethal weapon. "I thought he was a rare competitor," Parcells said. "I always knew—you could look at the national anthems before every game. He would stand right next to me on the left side. We were both a little suspicious, but we just did it. That was also his way of saying, 'Hey, I'm with you.' That's one of the things I remember most about him. I always felt he was with me. No matter

Six members of the Pro Football Hall of Fame, from left: Andy Robustelli, Sam Huff, Wellington Mara, Frank Gifford, Rosie Brown, and Tom Landry.

what—even when he went through some of his troubled times—I always felt like he was going to try to be with you. He was a great player, one of the great ones."

Simms is also one of Parcells's all-time favorite players. The quarterback was drafted in the first round in 1979, when Ray Perkins was the head coach. He stepped into the starting lineup in the sixth game of his rookie season and demonstrated that he would be an outstanding NFL quarterback. But in 1980 and 1981, his season was cut short by separated shoulders. Simms missed the entire 1982 season with a knee injury. In 1983 Parcells picked Scott Brunner as the starting quarterback over Simms. When Simms got a chance to play, he threw only thirteen passes before a fractured thumb knocked him out for the rest of the year. At that point no one knew if Simms would ever be a special quarterback.

But in 1984 he set team records for passes (533), completions (286), and yards (4,044), and he led the Giants to the playoffs. The following year he threw for 3,829 yards, and the Giants again played two postseason games. In 1986 Simms was magnificent, and the Giants won the Super Bowl. He and Parcells forged one of the most successful coach-quarterback partnerships in Giants history.

"We were walking out of the locker room before the first game of the 1984 season when he said to me, 'All right, Simms, let's go. Throw it down the field. If you don't throw two interceptions today, you're not trying hard enough,'" Simms said. "'Let's go. I want to see it.' He used to tell me that you have to take some chances. That was the easy part. I can live up to that."

Parcells has coached many outstanding quarterbacks since he had Simms, but the two men retain a special bond. "Phil was no box of chocolates," Parcells said. "He wasn't the easiest guy in those days. But he got to be the best for me. He was still trying to prove himself and it was a setback [when Parcells passed him over in '83]. And I know I bruised his ego and hurt his spirit. But at the end of the day, I was always glad I had him playing quarterback for me once we got by all that. I never went into a game saying I wish I had somebody else."

The Giants of that era are unanimous in their belief that Harry Carson belongs in the Hall of Fame. The great middle linebacker is a six-time finalist. Carson, an inside linebacker, was one of the best players in Giants history, a nine-time Pro Bowl selection in a career that stretched from 1976 to 1988. He led the Giants in tackles five times, was a two-time All-NFL selection, and, with his contemporary, George Martin, was a leader throughout his career, most notably on the 1986 Super Bowl champions. Parcells relied on Carson and Martin to police the locker room.

"'Straighten it out boys, I don't like it'—and they would do it," Parcells said. "Those are two of my favorites. I'd tell them, 'Go talk to this guy, straighten this guy out. Tell this guy to get a clue.' And there were some guys that wound up being good players.

"What people don't know is that Harry was an excellent practice player. He would practice his ass off, and George would practice his ass off. I was still making George do the same stuff rookies do when he was thirty-five. George was a special guy. I always have a special place in my heart for him. I think most people know that. He was like my pet."

Carson and Martin remain close friends today. Asked to give an example of Carson's leadership abilities, Martin recalls the scene in the locker room before the 49–3 rout of San Francisco in the 1986 postseason. "It's colder than a witch's you know what," Martin said. "Everybody's in the locker room, and it was like a trading market—'Give me gloves, give me socks, give me the hat, give me this.' And as we were deciding what we're going to wear because of the temperature, Harry Carson walks out of the training room. His locker was on the opposite side of the room. Harry had his shoulder pads on, he had his cut-off T-shirt, he had the abs showing, he was lubricated, so he's glistening. And he walks through there, and people looked at him like he was the black Adonis. And this hush came over the locker room. Everybody looked at him and said, 'That's the dress code right there.' It was absolutely phenomenal. Everybody took that crap off and threw it down. And you saw the results of it. That was a direct result of Harry Carson's leadership and him saying, 'You know what, weather doesn't matter. The circumstances do not matter. We got a game to play, and I'm coming ready to play, and here's my war garb.' And that's what it was. It was unbelievable."

Hein, Brown, Gifford, Taylor, Simms, and Carson are Giants' heroes of the past. Tiki Barber and Michael Strahan are today's idols. And with young quarterback Eli Manning on board, the team's tradition of greatness will continue.

Tiki Barber and Michael Strahan

When Giants fans look back on teams of the late 1990s and early 2000s, the players that will be foremost on their minds are Tiki Barber and Michael Strahan. They are the franchise's very best and most visible players of the new millennium. Both are record-holders, Pro Bowl players, and highly respected and well-liked teammates. They are active in charitable and community endeavors, are popular commercial spokesmen, and have distinguished themselves as broadcasters. In short they are big men in the biggest of cities.

For each there is irony in that statement. Because after their initial visits to New York, Strahan and Barber reached the same conclusion: It was not for them. Strahan was so intimidated he didn't leave his hotel room. Barber came for a visit and decided the city was everything bad he had heard it would be: too noisy, too crowded, too much like a place he didn't want to be.

Today, they laugh at their first impressions. Barber lives on the East Side of Manhattan with his wife, Ginny, and sons A. J. and Chason. He insists he is a New York lifer, unable to envision himself anywhere else. Strahan lived in the city for a year before settling in Montclair, a New Jersey suburb about 15 miles from Midtown.

On the field few NFL players are more accomplished. Strahan is the finest defensive end of his generation. Although he missed half of the 2004 season after undergoing surgery to repair a torn pectoral muscle, Strahan entered 2005 first among active players and twelfth in NFL history with 118.0 sacks (which became an official statistic in 1982). He holds the NFL single-season record with 22.5 sacks in 2001 and has played in six Pro Bowls.

"I have as much respect for Michael as I have for anybody," said Jim Fassel, head coach of the Giants from 1997 to 2003. "My last year, we were taking the field knowing we didn't have much of a chance. He still worked as hard as he always did and was a positive force and a positive influence. He was a positive guy. He practiced all the time. He didn't want to take practices off, never wanted to take plays off in a game. He got mad at me once because I took him out of a game when the game was over. He wanted to continue to play. He's one of the greatest I've ever been around."

Barber is single-handedly rewriting the Giants record book. In 2004 he had one of the best individual seasons in Giants history. Barber was selected to his first Pro Bowl after setting four significant team records: most single-seasons rushing yards (1,518), most career rushing yards (6,927), most single-season 100-yard games (9), and most yards from scrimmage in a season (2,096). He extended his franchise marks for receptions (474) and total yards (12,842).

"He is one of the greatest football players I have ever been around in my entire career," said general manager Ernie Accorsi, who has been in the NFL for thirty-four years. "And he has done something that, frankly, I have never seen close up. He has gotten better with age at a position that people feel has the shortest life expectancy. At running back players fall off quicker than probably most other positions, because all you have to do is lose a step and it makes a big difference. You can lose a little quickness because of the battering that a back takes on every play. But Tiki seems quicker and faster than he was four or five years ago. You have to admire his work ethic, his durability, his clutch play—there were periods when he just carried us. As an example of what a pro football player should be, he is everything you would ever want. He has got the character to go with it. It's just everything about him—he is a complete package."

Including a real New Yorker. Barber got his first taste of the city in early 1996, after his junior season at the University of Virginia. He and Ginny, then his girlfriend, bused up to the Big Apple to visit her sister. "She had a little studio apartment, which was something I had never seen before," Barber said. "It was snowing unbelievably. People were all over the place. The cabbies

Tiki Barber by the Numbers

Here are Tiki Barber's career statistics:

RUSHING

Year	Att	Yds	Avg	TD
1997	136	511	3.8	3
1998	52	166	3.2	0
1999	62	258	4.2	0
2000	213	1,006	4.7	8
2001	166	865	5.2	4
2002	304	1,387	4.6	11
2003	278	1,216	4.4	2
2004	322	1,518	4.7	13
TOTALS	1,533	6,927	4.5	41

RECEIVING

Year	No	Yds	Avg	TD
1997	34	299	8.8	1
1998	42	348	8.3	3
1999	66	609	9.2	2
2000	70	719	10.3	1
2001	72	577	8.0	0
2002	69	597	8.7	0
2003	69	461	6.7	1
2004	52	578	11.1	2
TOTALS	474	4,188	8.8	10

Tiki Barber is the Giants' career leader in rushing yards and total yards.

were nuts. You couldn't go anywhere. It was too busy for me. We got stuck here for three extra days. I'm from Virginia; I'm used to Charlottesville. It wasn't for me. I was a country boy. It was miserable. I told myself if I never go there again, it's too soon.

"Then, lo and behold, a year and a couple of months later, I get drafted here. I was nervous. But my wife was ecstatic. She always wanted to be a New Yorker. I came up early and got an apartment in Jersey City before we went to minicamp, because I wanted to learn about the place. I took the Path train into the city and experienced it a little bit. When Ginny graduated . . . we decided to move into the city. So my second year we moved to the Upper East Side to the same building I was in for six years. And I fell in love with New York. Now we're here for good. We bought a big place and we're staying. My brother [Ronde, a cornerback with the Tampa Bay Buccaneers] asks me, 'Do you want to come down to see me in Tampa?' I tell him, 'What the hell is there to do in Tampa?'"

Strahan had a similar experience. He was drafted in the second round in 1993, a year in which the Giants did not have a first-round draft choice. Soon after his selection, Strahan—who grew up for the most part in Germany and played collegiate football at Texas Southern in Houston—traveled to New York to check it out.

"I didn't hate it. I was scared of it," Strahan said. "I stayed in the Marriott Marquis in Times Square. The only time I left the room was when somebody came to pick me up. I was scared to go out. I had never seen anything like it. I'd look out my window at two or three in the morning—I was awake because I'd been in the room all day and had all that energy—and people were walking in the street like ants. I thought, 'If I go outside, I'm going to get robbed, shot, or killed.' But New York is so far from that. I love it. I don't want to be anywhere else.

"I look back now, and I laugh at it. But can you imagine coming from Germany and going to Houston, which I thought was the fastest city in the world? It never stopped. Then you come to New York, which makes Houston seem like a sleeping baby. It was hard to adjust to. It took me time to get used to the pace."

Strahan also had some early adjustments to make on the field. He missed much of his rookie season after suffering a foot injury in the preseason. In 1996 Strahan moved from right to left end and saw his sack total drop from 7.5 to 5.0. He did not hit a double-digit sack total in any of his first four seasons. But in 1997 he began to hit his stride. Strahan totaled 29 sacks the next two years and played in the Pro Bowl each of the next three seasons. After missing out in 2000, the year the Giants played in the Super Bowl, Strahan again went to Hawaii three years in a row.

To say Strahan has exceeded his goals is the understatement of the young century. "When I got here in '93, I was hoping to make it to '94," Strahan said. "So to be sitting here all these years later and to be the elder on this team is pretty amazing. In this day and age, to be with one team for so long is a feat within itself."

Just as their feelings for New York developed similarly, so did the football careers of Barber and Strahan. Barber was also a second-round selection (the thirty-sixth choice overall, four spots ahead of where Strahan was taken) in 1997. Fassel, who had recently been hired, and the general manager, George Young, considered grabbing him with the seventh pick on the first round, but instead opted for wide receiver Ike Hilliard.

"At the end of the day, Ike was graded just a little bit higher on the board," Fassel said. "Doing the research and looking between our first pick and our second pick at how many teams would be interested in a running back—there weren't a lot of teams that were going to take one. And the teams we thought might take a running back were looking more for a big, powerful back. I felt like we had a good chance this way. We could have taken either guy. But the grades said Ike, and I didn't want to go away from the grades. A lot of people didn't agree with me—they said Tiki wouldn't last [in the draft]. I said based upon the needs everybody has, he'll still be there. But it was a risk. That made me more nervous than anything. I was sweating until he was still there at our second pick."

Barber, who is 5' 10" and 200 pounds, was typecast as a third-down back and return man. Like Strahan's, his initial goal was simply to stick around for a couple of years. "I think everyone is that way," Barber said. "If you're an elite guy coming out of college, you aspire to these great things. But I was typecast before I even took one snap. I just wanted to have a respectful career. I didn't necessarily care what I achieved, other than winning games and being someone to rely on. Now I have a lot of the records in the book, I've been to a Super Bowl, and now I've made the Pro Bowl. It's weird to think about, because a lot of people look at me in a certain light that I don't see myself in."

As a rookie, Barber rushed for 511 yards and caught 34 passes. The next two years, he caught 108 passes but rushed for a total of only 424 yards. Barber broke out in his fourth season in 2000, when he rushed for 1,006 yards, the first of four 1,000-yard seasons in five years. He never caught fewer than 69 passes in any of those years. At the conclusion of the 2004 season, Barber was the only active player, and just the third overall, to lead a franchise in both rushing yards and receptions. The others were Hall of Famer Walter Payton (16,726 rushing yards and 492 catches for Chicago) and James Wilder (5,957 rushing yards and 430 catches for Tampa Bay).

"That means a lot to me, considering he [Payton] was my idol growing up and the kind of player he was," Barber said. "It is an honor and it's an accomplishment. But it's not something I set out to do. It kind of happened. Circumstances have been right for me over the years.

"A lot of people don't realize it, but after three years in the NFL, I probably didn't have a thousand yards rushing [he had 935]," Barber said. "Three years into my career, I wasn't the guy, I wasn't the every-down back, I wasn't playing a ton of time. Then I finally got my opportunity, and I've taken advantage of it in a lot of ways."

Although he sometimes used Barber sparingly early in the back's career, Fassel said he wasn't worried about Barber's staying power or his productivity. "A lot of people think small backs won't last," Fassel said. "The opposite is true. The guys that are quick and on the smallish side, they're the guys that last the longest. The bigger guys don't last as long, because when they run they take a pounding continuously. I never questioned Tiki's durability and longevity. He's a tough guy. He's played through some injuries.

"Did I think, when his career was over, that he would be one of the New York Giants' leaders in those statistical categories? Yeah. But at the time I didn't fully appreciate what Tiki would mean as a team member, what he would mean to the team as a person. I knew he was a great guy, but you never know how that's going to be. He's a professional, he's smart, and he'll make the change. I had faith in him."

Not surprisingly, the two accomplished players who had similar experiences and have shared space in the same locker room for so many years are friends and admirers of each other.

"He has been like the heart and soul of the team just for the way that he goes out every week," Strahan said. "And he's been consistent and he runs hard. And as a defensive player, when you sit on the sidelines and you watch the offense, you know you can always count on Tiki to give you what you want or what you need as a team, to give you a boost. And I think that's the mark of a great player. Not go out having one good year, not having a few good games. It's having guys count on your productivity every week, and you give it to them. That's a testament to how hard he works in the off-season and how much he wants to be successful on and off the field."

Barber is equally complimentary toward Strahan. "When I think about Michael, what stands out is his accountability to everyone," Barber said. "Before every game, even when he was hurt, he goes around and he basically touches your hand or hits you on the head and says, 'Get ready, because I'm going to be here for you for the whole game.' And he's a competitor. People don't give him credit for [being] as complete a player as he is. They talk about his sacks, but he's a great player against the run, too. So he's done all the requisite things to be one of the greats in this game as a defensive end. It's a privilege to play with a guy like that. Because you know he's never taken practice off, you know he's not going to lie down and quit during the game. You have to respect that because you can't say that about everybody."

Michael Strahan by the Numbers

Here are Michael Strahan's career statistics:

Year	Tackles	Sacks	Int	Yds	TD
1993	9	1.0	0	0	0
1994	40	4.5	0	0	0
1995	58	7.5	2	56	0
1996	63	5.0	0	0	0
1997	68	14.0	0	0	0
1998	67	15.0	1	24	1
1999	58	5.5	1	44	1
2000	66	9.5	0	0	0
2001	73	22.5	0	0	0
2002	71	11.0	0	0	0
2003	75	18.5	0	0	0
2004	35	4.0	0	0	0
TOTALS	683	118.0	4	124	2

This is not to suggest that the Barber-Strahan relationship has always been perfect. In the months prior to the 2002 season, they had an ugly and much-publicized spat. Strahan was in the midst of contract negotiations and made some statements Barber didn't care for. Barber made the mistake of voicing his opinions in a newspaper. That prompted some angry exchanges, both publicly

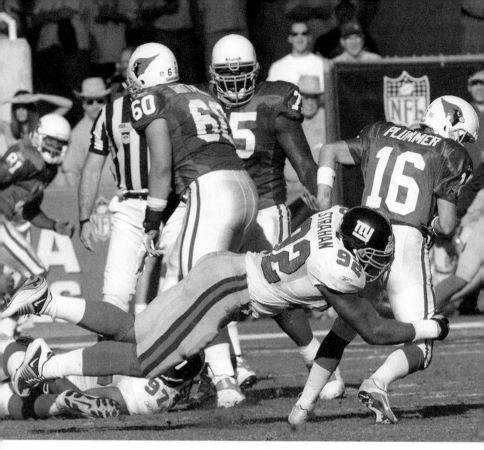

Michael Strahan (92) holds the NFL single-season record for sacks.

and privately. Today both consider the disagreement to be ancient history, and they are close friends.

"Our relationship is great now," Barber said. "We have an understanding about what happened. We're both good guys. We had a philosophical difference. It got aired because of my mistakes, instead of being handled privately. And it became a big issue. But the weird thing is when it actually should have come to a head, it didn't. Because we were man enough to put it behind us and realize that the best thing for this team is that we play together, to cooperate. And I know that Michael's a good guy; he's a good friend. There's no need to have this kind of argument or kind of disagreement. Over time you realize, we like each other. We hang, we're cool, we're buddies."

"I get along great with Tiki," Strahan said. "A lot of times when somebody calls you and they say, 'This guy turned down that and this is what he said about you,' and you don't go to the guy to find out exactly what it was, things get misconstrued. I can understand where Tiki was coming from because I've been on the other end of that, and I know how the media can be deceptive because they want to get a story out of it. At the same time I'm not dumb. You think I'm going to go out and get even by hurting Tiki Barber [as some suggested he might in training camp]? I want to win, and Tiki's one of the key guys."

With the fracture healed, Strahan and Barber returned to their roles as invaluable players, leaders, teammates, and friends, putting together similarly brilliant legacies for a storied franchise.

"To be here for so long with one team and to do so well for this one team—and in the toughest place to play in the league— it's something I'm proud of," Strahan said. "But until the last few years, I never really thought about leaving a legacy here. I remember them retiring Phil and Lawrence's jerseys, and that's what I want. When I walk out wearing that number 92 for the last time, I don't want anybody else to wear it. I want that to be it. Hopefully, I'll do my best to make that happen. It takes a lot of work to get the respect and the results that those guys had. Hopefully, I can get to the point where it's even considered and I'll be happy."

"I am proud that I have been able to do it for so long," Barber said. "It's easy to do something great once, to have a great game or a great year. But I think true greatness is determined by consistency and doing those things over and over and over again. I think when my career is said and done that's what people will say about me, 'Yeah, he had his faults sometimes, but overall he was a consistent player for us. He helped us win and did great things over and over again.' That's what I am most proud of, because when I came in this league I was going to be just a nobody."

He's a big somebody now, just like his friend Michael Strahan. And they're both big men in the greatest city in the world.

Who would have thought?

About the Author

Michael Eisen has seen more than 300 Giants game in the last twenty years. He covered the team for two New Jersey newspapers for fourteen years before joining the Giants organization in 2000.